AF600406

THE CATHOLIC UNIVERSITY OF AMERICA
CANON LAW STUDIES
No. 154

The Time and Place for the Celebration of Marriage

AN HISTORICAL SYNOPSIS
AND COMMENTARY

BY THE

REV. EDWARD JOHN DODWELL, Ph.D., S.T.B., J.C.L.
Priest of the Diocese of Savannah-Atlanta

A DISSERTATION

Submitted to the Faculty of Canon Law of the Catholic University of America in Partial Fulfillment of the Requirements for the Degree of

DOCTOR OF CANON LAW

THE CATHOLIC UNIVERSITY OF AMERICA
WASHINGTON, D. C.
1942

NIHIL OBSTAT:

CLEMENS V. BASTNAGEL, S.T.L., J.U.D.,
Censor Deputatus.

Washingtonii, D. C., die XXIV Maii, 1942.

IMPRIMATUR:

✠ GERALDUS P. O'HARA, D.D., J.U.D.,
Episcopus Savannensis-Atlantensis.

Savannae, die XXXI Maii, 1942.

PRINTED IN THE UNITED STATES OF AMERICA
BY THE WATKINS PRINTING CO., BALTIMORE

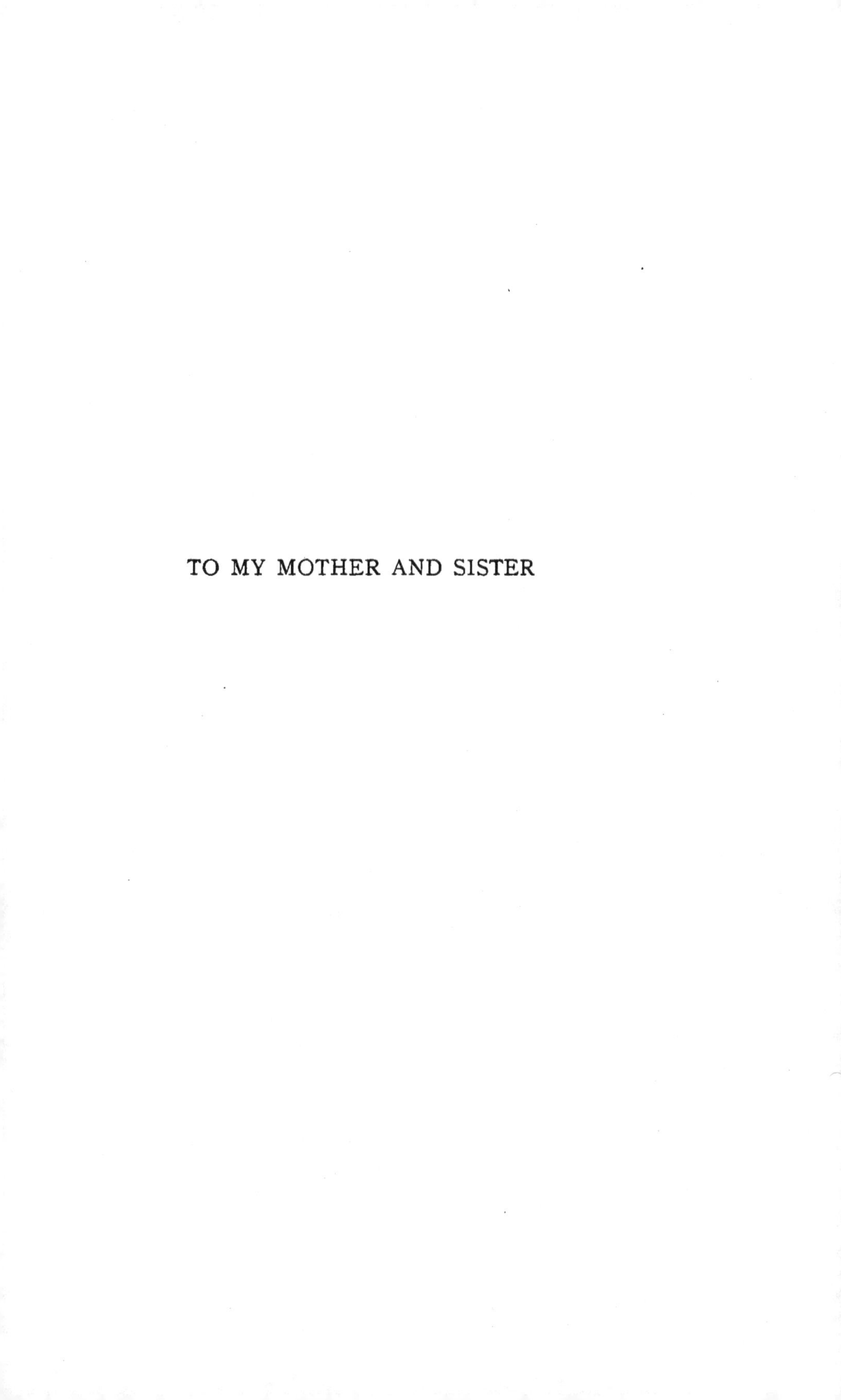

TO MY MOTHER AND SISTER

TABLE OF CONTENTS

FOREWORD

The title of this dissertation is taken from the rubric, *De tempore et loco celebrationis matrimonii,* which is prefixed to canons 1108 and 1109 of the Code of Canon Law. The fact that the Code brings these two distinct concepts under one heading is sufficient reason for treating them together in a single work.[1]

In the first part of this work, namely the Historical Synopsis, the history of legislation concerning the forbidden times, and the place for the celebration of marriage, will be traced from the early days of the Church to the promulgation of the Code. However, in order to understand adequately the historical outline of legislation forbidding the solemnization of marriage during the closed time, and of that prescribing that the marriages of Catholics be celebrated in church, a general idea at least must be had of the marriage ceremony itself. For this purpose a chapter on the history of the marriage rite with special emphasis on the Nuptial Blessing will precede the historical notions of the time and place for the celebration of marriage. In this preliminary chapter on the history of the marriage blessing the liturgical form of marriage alone will be treated to the exclusion of the juridical form, namely that required for validity. Since canon 1109 treats, in paragraph three, of the place for mixed marriages, and refers to Canon 1102, § 2, which legislates against the use of sacred rites in mixed marriages, the final chapter of the Historical Synopsis will trace the development of legislation concerning the celebration of mixed marriages in so far as the place of celebration and the rites employed in celebration are concerned.

The Canonical Commentary, in a manner analogous to the Historical Synopsis, before treating the legislation of canons 1108 and 1109, will discuss the liturgical form of marriage. This will

[1] Of all the pre-Code writers Gasparri seems to stand alone in grouping these two concepts under one heading, *De tempore ac loco quo matrimonium celebrare licet.* Cf. Gasparri, *Tractatus Canonicus de Matrimonio* (2 vols., Parisiis, 1904), nn. 1245-1271. This work will be cited hereafter as *De Matrimonio* (ed. 1904).

entail a treatment of canons 1100 and 1101. The prescription of canon 1102, § 2, which forbids all sacred rites at mixed marriages, will be discussed, and only in so far as it refers to the marriages of canon 1109, § 3, which commands that mixed marriages be performed outside of church. Hence in the preliminary chapter of the Canonical Commentary the liturgical form of marriage alone will be discussed, and only in so far as it refers to the marriages of Catholics. The final chapter of the work, although primarily concerned with the liturgical form in mixed marriages, will treat in passing the law of canon 1102, § 1, which prescribes that the juridical form must be employed in the celebration of mixed marriages, thus abolishing the so-called "passive assistance" at mixed marriages.

The writer takes this opportunity to express publicly his sincere gratitude to his Excellency, the Most Rev. Gerald P. O'Hara, D.D., J.U.D., for making it possible for him to pursue graduate studies in the School of Canon Law of the Catholic University of America. He wishes also to thank the Faculty of the School of Canon Law for their helpful direction and kind assistance.

PART I

HISTORICAL SYNOPSIS

Chapter I

THE HISTORY OF THE MARRIAGE BLESSING

Article I—Roman Marriage Customs and Their Influence on Christian Marriage

To understand adequately the history of the Christian marriage ceremony some knowledge must be had of the Roman marriage customs which existed at the time when Christianity came into being. By this time the older formal institutions of Roman marriage law were practically extinct. These forms, namely, *usus, confarreatio* and *co-emptio,* which brought the wife under the *manus* of the husband, were almost non-existent at the end of the classical period of Roman Law. In the words of Corbett, "In the Rome of the classical jurists, *manus* is a matter of legal archeology." [1] In another passage the same author states that, from the legal point of view, marriage in this period of Roman Law is almost, if not altogether, a formless transaction; and that a knowledge of the religious and secular ceremonies of Roman marriage must be gleaned from non-juristic literature. [2]

Hence it is safe to assert with Watkins that the marriages of Christians were not much concerned with any of these three ancient forms which effected a *conventio in manum.*[3] Therefore in estimating the influence of Roman custom on the Christian marriage ceremony, an examinaiton must be made of the Roman ceremonies actually current in the first centuries of Christianity. In other words, it is with the usual ceremonies of marriages contracted without *manus* that this article is concerned. Watkins gives a very complete description of the Roman marriage ceremony.[4] This ceremony comprises really two sets of ceremonies, the ceremonies of the betrothal and those of the wedding.

[1] Corbett, *The Roman Law of Marriage* (Oxford: Clarendon Press, 1930), p. 91.

[2] *Op. cit.,* p. 68.

[3] Watkins, *Holy Matrimony* (New York, 1895), p. 82.

[4] *Op. cit.,* pp. 83-86. Cf. also Joyce, *Christian Marriage* (Sheed and Ward: London and New York, 1933), p. 41; Duchesne, *Christian Worship*

THE BETROTHAL. Among the Romans marriage was usually preceded by the *sponsalia,* or betrothal. It was customary on some day before the wedding itself for the parties interested to meet at the house of the bride's father to arrange the contract of betrothal. The contract was written on tables *(tabulae sponsales)* and signed by both the betrothed parties in the presence of witnesses. At the same time the future husband bestowed the *arrhae,* or bridal gifts, on his intended wife. These gifts were the *donatio propter nuptias.* Among them was probably included the *annulus pronubus* which the man placed on the woman's finger. The kiss and the mutual hand clasp *(conluctatio manuum)* concluded the ceremonies of the *sponsalia.*

THE WEDDING. The auspices having been consulted and a suitable day having been chosen, the actual marriage ceremony took place. The bride wore the dress of married women, and the veil, called the *flammeum* because of its bright yellow color. Both bride and bridegroom wore a crown of flowers. This is the origin of the crowning of the bride and groom which still forms a striking feature in marriages of the Eastern Church. After the ceremony followed the formal reading of the *tabulae nuptiales,* which were then signed by the parties and witnesses. The *deductio in domum,* or the leading of the bride in triumphal procession to the home of her husband, formed the final incident of the marriage ceremonies.

These in brief are the Roman marriage customs in vogue in the early centuries of Christianity. But to what extent did the Christians adopt or modify the marriage customs which they found in use around them? There was nothing to hinder them from changing these ceremonies, since, as has been shown above, marriage in this period of history was practically a formless transaction among the Romans, and none of these customs was obligatory by law. Yet men are unlikely to change age old customs unless forced to do so. Most of these ceremonies were harmless enough, and were in great part retained.

(London and New York, 1903), pp. 433-434. The latter, however, includes the *confarreatio,* or sacrifice to Jupiter, which, as Corbett shows (*op. cit.,* p. 78), had been restricted by the Christian times to the marriages of priests.

Arguing from the fact that some Christian writers used the term *desponsatio* to signify the actual marriage, and *sponsa* to denote the wife until the common life had actually begun, Joyce is of the opinion that the Christians were accustomed to combine the ceremonies of betrothal and marriage, and that at the *desponsatio* the priestly blessing was given. Thus *desponsatio* would denote the actual marriage in the eyes of the Church, and *nuptiae* would mean the celebrations which took place later when the bride was brought to her husband's house. In the appendix to his work he gives a number of texts from authors ranging from Tertullian to Panormitanus in support of his opinion. He admits, however, that the practice was not uniform, and that in many passages the word *desponsatio* retains its old sense of betrothal.[5]

From what has been seen it may be concluded that the marriage of the early Christians was simply the marriage of Roman law, and especially of Roman custom, with a Christian prayer of benediction somewhere added.[6] It will be the purpose of the following article to show the importance of this benediction, which was the blessing of the priest; and to adduce testimonies to show that this priestly blessing, although not required for validity, existed in the celebration of Christian marriage from the early days of the Church.

Article II—The Priestly Blessing in General During the First Ten Centuries

Christ raised marriage to the dignity of a sacrament, and the Apostles and the Fathers of the Church recognized its sacred character.[7] Because of its sacred character Christian marriage

[5] *Christian Marriage,* Appendix, pp. 600-601; also p. 46 and notes 3 and 4. Cf. also Esmein, *Le Mariage en Droit Canonique,* (12. ed., 2 vols. [Vol. I rev. by R. Génestal, 1929, Vol. II rev. by R. Gênestal & J. Dauvillier 1935], Recueil Sirey: Paris, 1929-1935), I, 112-113. Hereafter this work will be cited as Esmein, *Le Mariage.*

[6] Watkins, *Holy Matrimony,* p. 90; Wernz, *Ius Decretalium,* Tomus IV, *Ius Matrimoniale Ecclesiae Catholicae* (2. ed., Prati: *Pars Prima,* 1911; *Pars Secunda,* 1912), n. 154, p. 202. Hereafter this work will be cited as *Ius Matrimoniale.*

[7] For proofs of the sacramental character of Christian marriage drawn from Scripture and the Fathers see Joyce, *Christian Marriage,* pp. 156-167.

belongs within the province of the Church, and for this reason the Church has always forbidden clandestine marriages, namely, those entered into without her intervention.[8] This intervention is shown from the fact that at least from the third century, and very probably from apostolic times, Christians usually received the priestly blessing when they were married.[9] This is proved by the numerous texts which mention the priestly blessing in connection with Christian marriage.

It will be the purpose of this article, then, to show by a number of testimonies that practically from the earliest days of Christianity, a sacred rite, at least the priestly blessing, accompanied the celebration of Christian marriage. Whether this sacred rite included the celebration of Mass, and more particularly of the Nuptial Mass, will be considered in the next article.

The oldest genuine testimony concerning the Church's intervention in the celebration of Christian marriage is found in the letter of St. Ignatius, Bishop of Antioch (70-107), to Polycarp: "It is fitting that those who enter marriage, should do so with the advice of the bishop, so that the marriage may be according to the Lord and not according to the desires of the flesh."[10] It is true that this text unsupported would not indicate a sacred ceremony in use at the marriages of the early Christians; but that such a ceremony existed, at least from the third century, is clear from the writings of Tertullian. The best known passage is found in his *Ad Uxorem* (*circa* 197): "Where shall we find power to describe the happiness of that marriage, which the church arranges, the oblation confirms, the benediction seals, the angels proclaim, and the

[8] Conc. Trident., sess XXIV, *de ref. matrim.*, c. 1: "Tametsi dubitandum non est, clandestina matrimonia, libero contrahentitum consensu facta, rata et vera esse matrimonia, quamdiu ecclesia ea irrita non fecit . . . nihilominus sancta Dei ecclesia ex iustissimis causis illa semper detestata est atque prohibuit."

[9] Benedictus XIV, *De Synodo Dioecesana* (2 vols., Romae, 1767), lib. VIII, cap. 12, n. 3; Joyce, *Christian Marriage*, p. 163; Wernz, *Ius Matrimoniale*, nn. 154-155, n. 189.

[10] C. 5—Migne, *Patrologiae Cursus Completus, Series Graeca* (161 vols., Parisiis, 1856-1866), V. 963. Hereafter this collection will be cited as *MPG.*

Father ratifies."[11] The same writer, in his Montanist treatise *De Monogomia* (*circa* 217), implies that marriage was ordinarily sought from the bishop and clergy.[12] These two testimonies combinded seem to indicate that the clergy had a part in the preliminaries to the marriage and in the actual celebration of the marriage. Another text of the same writer indicates how severely reprobated were clandestine unions, entered into without the approval and cooperation of the Church.[13]

A letter of Pope Siricius (384-399), the authenticity of which cannot be questioned,[14] gives an idea of the veneration in which the priestly blessing was held. The Pope, on being asked whether a woman who had been espoused *(desponsata)* to one man could break her pledge and enter a valid marriage with another, replied:

> We forbid in every possible way that this should be done. For if the blessing which the priest gives to the woman who is about to marry *(nupturae)* be violated by a breach of her vow, the faithful regard such a violation as a kind of sacrilege.[15]

St Ambrose, attacking marriages between Christians and unbelievers, says: "For when the marriage itself must be sanctified

[11] Lib. III, c. 9—Migne, *Patrologiae Cursus Completus, Series Latina* 221 vols., Parisiis, 1844-1864), I, 1302. Hereafter this collection will be cited as *MPL.*

[12] C. XI—*MPL,* II, 943.

[13] *De Pudicitia,* c. 4—*MPL,* II, 987.

[14] Hinschius, *Decretales Pseudo-Isidorianae et Capitula Angilramni,* (Lipsiae, 1863, p. xvciii: "De Siricii epistolis tribus ex Hispana desumptis . . . controversia nulla est."

[15] *Epistola Decretalis Siricii ad Himerium Terraconensem,* c. 4—*MPL,* XIII, 1136—Jaffé, *Regesta Pontificium Romanorum ab Condita Ecclesia ad Annum Post Christum MCXCVIII* (2. ed., correctam et auctam auspiciis G. Wattenbach curaverunt S. Loewenfeld, F. Kaltenbrunner, P. Ewald, 2 vols., Lipsiae, 1885-1888), n. 255. This work hereafter will be cited as Jaffé. Joyce, in accordance with his theory already mentioned (*supra,* p. 3), renders *desponsata* as "a woman whose marriage was as yet unconsummated," and *nupturae* as "a woman who is about to enter on conjugal life." (*Christian Marriage,* p. 163 and note 1). Cf. Gratian's *dictum* on c. 50 C. XXVII, q. 2 (the letter of Pope Siricius), which seems to favor Joyce's interpretation of this text.

by the priestly veiling and blessing, how can that be called marriage where there is no agreement of faith." [16]

Pope Innocent I (401-417), in one of his letters, writes: "We are taught that the blessing bestowed on the bridal pair by the priest is an observance of a law instituted long since by God." [17]

The *Statuta Ecclesiae Antiqua,* a collection of canons of Greek and Gallic councils and of letters of the popes, compiled at Arles around the end of the fifth century, mentions the blessing which the bride and groom receive from the priest. Out of reverence for this blessing they are to forgo the use of marriage until the following day.[18]

But it is evident that the priestly blessing was not always received, since not a few enactments are found forbidding clandestine marraiges and prescribing the priestly blessing. For example, the Council of Verno decreed that all marriages should be performed publicly.[19]

The capitularies of the Frankish kings are strong in their insistence on the priestly blessing. The capitulary of Aix-la-Chapelle in the year 789 incorporates the letter of Pope Siricius into its decrees.[20] The capitulary of the year 802 prescribing pre-nuptial

[16] *Ep. XIX* (ad Vigil.)—*MPL,* XVI, 985. The words *velamine sacerdotali* used by St. Ambrose are an allusion to the practice of covering the spouses with a veil during the marriage blessing. For an indication of the use of this ceremony in France and Mexico until recent times cf. Villien, *The History and Liturgy of the Sacraments* (English translation by H. W. Edwards, Burns, Oates & Washbourne: London, 1932), p. 316; also S.R.C., *Mexicana,* 27 feb. 1886—*Fontes,* n. 6172.

[17] *Ep. II* (ad Victricium)—*MPL,* XX, 475—Jaffé, 286.

[18] Mansi, *Sacrorum Conciliorum Nova et Amplissima Collectio* (53 vols in 59, Parisiis, 1901-1927), III, 952. Hereafter quoted as Mansi.

[19] *Capitula Synodi Vernensis,* c. 15; "Ut Omnes homines laici publicas nuptias faciant tam nobiles, quam ignobiles."—*Monumenta Germaniae Historica* (hereafter *MGH), Legum Sectio II,* Tom. I, *Capitularia Regum Francorum* (ed. Alfredus Boretius, Hanoverae, 1883), 36.

[20] *Capitulare Aquisgranense sive Capitulare Primum Anni 789,* Capit. 51—*MGH,* Leges, I (ed. Pertz, Hanoverae, 1925), 62.

investigation in order to prevent incestuous marriages, commands also that marriages be blessed by the priest.[21]

Provincial councils, also, at this same period, are insistent on the priestly blessing. The Council of Rouen in the year 1072 prescribes that the bride and groom be fasting and be blessed by a priest who is fasting.[22] The Council of London in the year 1175 commanded that all marriages should be public and should be blessed by the priest.[23]

To sum up the evidence of the first thousand years of Christianity, it may be asserted that from the earliest ages of Christianity the priestly blessing, although not required as a condition for validity, was the usual accompaniment of marriage between Christians. The Decree of Gratian gives several texts showing the practice of the first thousand years of Christianity.[24] The classical text concerning the sacred rites used at Christian marriage (c. 3, XXX, q. 5) namely, the reply of Pope Nicholas I (858-867) to the Bulgarian Christians, will be considered in the following article.

Article III—Historical Notes on the Nuptial Mass and Blessing

It has been shown in the preceding article that, from the earliest ages of the Church, the priestly blessing was the usual accompaniment of Christian marriage. The question now arises: when the Christians of the early centuries came before the priest or

21 *Capitulare Primum a. 802 Karoli Magni—MGH, Legum Sectio II,* Tom. II (ed. Boretius, 1883), 98.

22 Conc. Rotomagense c. 15—Mansi XX, 38.

23 "Nullus fidelis, cuiuscumque conditionis sit, occulte nuptias faciat, sed benedictione accepta a sacerdote, publice nubat in Domino."—Mansi XXII, 151. This text, which Gratian (c. 2 C. XXX, q. 5) attributes to Pope Hormisdas (514-523), is shown by Berardi to be spurious. He says that Burchard of Worms took it from the Capitularies of the Frankish kings and ascribed it to Pope Hormisdas. Cf. Berardi, *Gratiani Canones Genuini ab Apocryphis Discreti* (4 vols., Venetiis, 1777), II, 386. Hereafter Berardi's work will be cited as *Gratiani canones.*

24 Cc. 1, 2, 3, 5, C. XXX, q. 5; c. 19, C. XXXV, q. 19.

bishop to contract or declare their marriage, and to ask the Church's blessing on it, was this blessing given during the Holy Sacrifice of the Mass? We have no definite proof that such was the case in the first four or five centuries. It can be asserted almost with certainty that there was no special Mass *pro sponsis* like ours. The only possible allusion in the early centuries to a Mass in connection with the celebration of marriage is the passage of Tertullian's *Ad Uxorem* already alluded to.[25] Some authors take the word *oblatio* in this passage as referring to the Holy Sacrifice, but all are not in agreement on this point.[26]

Whatever may be the interpretation of this passage, it is certain that a special *Missa pro Sponsis* existed in the sixth century and possibly earlier. For the Leonine Sacramentary, which dates from the sixth century and is no doubt based on an older tradition, contains a marriage formula entitled, *Incipit velation nuptialis.* This sacramentary contains five prayers and a preface for the *velatio nuptialis.*[27]

The Nuptial Mass is also met with in the Gelasian and Gregorian Sacramentaries. Though their formulae differ con-

[25] Lib. II, c. 9: "Unde sufficiamus ad enarrandam felicitatem eius matrimonii, quod Ecclesia conciliat, et *confirmat oblatio,* et obsignat benedictio, angeli renuntiant, Pater rato habet." — *MPL,* I, 1302. Cf. *supra,* p. 4.

[26] Joyce interprets *oblatio* as referring to the Holy Sacrifice. Cf. *Christian Marriage,* p. 162. Villien also inclines to this view. Cf. *History and Liturgy of the Sacraments,* p. 307. Cappello *(Tractatus Canonico-Moralis de Sacramentis,* Vol. III, *De Matrimonio* [4. ed., Taurinorum Augustae: Marietti, 1930], n. 658*)* takes the word *oblatio* as referring to the offering of prayers. The writer of the article on Marriage in the *Dictionary of Christian Antiquities (*[ed. Smith & Cheetham, 2 vols., London, 1908,], II, 1106, col. 2 and note*)* refers the word *oblatio* to prayers and alms offered by the spouses through the ministry of the priest, which, he says, correspond to the *arrhae* or marriage gifts of the pagans. In his footnote he censures Dr. Döllinger for translating *Ecclesia conciliat, confirmat obliatio* by, "the marriage was concluded by the bishop or presbyter uniting the betrothed, and confirmed by the offering of the Holy Sacrifice," and remarks: "It is impossible to believe that this is the meaning of *confirmat oblatio* in this passage."

[27] The text of this sacramentary is found in *MPL,* LV, 130-131. For the meaning of *velatio nuptialis* cf. supra p. 6, note 16.

siderably from that of the Leonine Sacramentary, the general arrangement of the office is the same. The *Sacramentarium Gallicanum,* or Bobbio Missal, does not contain a Nuptial Mass. That the Nuptial Mass, however, was known on the other side of the Alps is shown by the existence in Gaul of manuscripts of the Roman Sacramentaries.[28] Also, it is a well known fact that Charlemagne, wishing to establish the Roman liturgy in Gaul, received from Pope Hadrian (772-795) a copy of a the Gregorian Sacramentary.[29]

It is evident, however, that some Christians must have neglected the use of the Nuptial Mass and Blessing, for Bishop Jonas of Orleans, at the beginning of the ninth century, rebukes those who deprive themselves of the blessing with which God sanctified the union of the first human couple, and of that which is *now* given to the spouses in church by the priest, in accordance with the authority of the holy canons and the custom of the Roman Church. It is this neglect which has introduced the reprehensible custom according to which the bride and groom very rarely receive the prescribed blessing during the celebration of Mass.[30]

The blessing alluded to by Bishop Jonas usually took place somewhere between the *Libera nos* and the *Pax Domini,* although there were exceptions to this rule, the blessing sometimes being given only after Mass was completed.[31] At any rate, somewhere in the ceremony the Nuptial Blessing properly so called was given. The sacramentaries and ordos, then, attest to the existence of a special Nuptial Blessing given in immediate connection with the Mass, as early as the sixth century, if not earlier. This Mass in the Roman books was a special votive Mass. In fact, the Introit to the Mass of the *Sacramentarium Gregorianum* was the same

[28] Cf. Martène, *De Antiquis Ecclesiae Ritibus* (3 vols., Rotomagi, 1700-1702), II, *Ordo* I, p. 614, for the marriage Mass of the Gelasian Missal.

[29] A redaction of this sacramentary by Alcuin is found in *MPL,* LXXVIII, 25-239.

[30] *De Institutione Laicali,* II, ii.—*MPL,* CVI, 170.

[31] Villien, *History and Liturgy of the Sacraments,* pp. 318-320. Cf. also the *ordines* reproduced by Martene, *De Antiquis Ecclesiae Ritibus,* II, 616 ff.

as that of our votive Mass *pro sponso et sponsa.*[32] It would seem that in Gaul the Mass used was a votive Mass of the Blessed Trinity, with the addition of the special marriage blessing.[33]

Mention was made on page 7 of the letter of Pope Nicholas I (858-867). In this letter is found one of the best and most complete descriptions of the marriage ceremonies in vogue in the Roman Church in the middle of the ninth century.[34]

The rites described by the Pope may be divided into four stages: 1. the betrothal in view of a future marriage, contracted with the consent of parents or legal guardians; 2. the rite of *desponsatio,* when the *arrhae* were given, the ring placed on the bride's finger, and the deed of settlement delivered to her; 3. the Mass at which the pair received the Church's blessing, while a veil was held over their heads; 4. the crowning while they left the Church to enter on conjugal life.[35]

With the exception of the *velatio nuptialis* and the crowning *(de Ecclesia egressi coronas in capitibus gestant),* which latter still occupies an important place in the Byzantine rite, the ceremonies described by Pope Nicholas are essentially the same as those of the Latin rite today. The modern ceremony, however, combines the betrothal and marriage ceremony into one. Today the marriage ceremony begins with the declaration of consent, which from the circumstances becomes a *promissio de praesenti*. Then follows the *subarrhatio,* performed by the groom with a ring previously blessed. This ceremony is followed in some countries, Ireland for example, by the conveyance of a medal or a piece of money, which represents the bestowal of the dowry. Then follows the

[32] Villien, *op. cit.,* p. 310.

[33] Villien, *op. cit.,* p. 312.

[34] *Ad Consulta Bulgarorum,* c. III—*MPL, CXIX,* 979-980—Jaffé, 2812. Joyce (*Christian Marriage,* pp. 599-600) has reproduced the Latin text of the Pope's letter.

[35] Joyce (*Christian Marriage,* p. 47) says the second stage was considered as the actual marriage, since the first is particularly specified as being a promise of a future union. The second stage (*desponsatio*) would be followed immediately by the Nuptial Mass; but if the parties were under the age prescribed by law, this would be postponed until the time had come for conjugal life to begin.

Nuptial Mass during which the wedded couple receive the Nuptial Blessing.

The Nuptial Blessing, which is contained in the Roman Missal, is the marriage blessing *par excellence,* and, though it is not of obligation, the Church desires all her children to receive it. But whether the Nuptial Mass and Blessing take place or are omitted, the marriage ceremony contained in the Roman Ritual or an approved diocesan ritual must be employed at all Catholic marriages, as will be seen in the Canonical Commentary of this dissertation. This ceremony contains what may be called the simple Nuptial Blessing or the Ritual Blessing contained in the words, *"Ego coniungo vos in matrimonium. In nomine Patris, et Filii,* ✠ *et Spiritus Sancti. Amen.* In order to facilitate an understanding of what will be said in other parts of this work, the following article will give a few historical notes on this Ritual Blessing.

Article IV—Historical Notes on the Ritual Blessing

In the previous article a distinction was made between the Nuptial Blessing and the Blessing of the Ritual, and it was noted that the latter is contained in the words, *"Ego coniungo vos, etc."* and must be imparted at all Catholic marriages. If the Nuptial Mass follows, the solemn or Nuptial Blessing is given during it. This blessing ordinarily is not separated from the Nuptial Mass.[36]

There can be no doubt that the Nuptial Blessing contained in the Roman Missal is the solemn official marriage blessing of the Church, but it is equally evident that our present formula of the Ritual also contains a blessing. Feije demonstrates at length that this formula, or a similar one found in diocesean rituals, is a true blessing, and that the Church considers it as such.[37] He also shows

[36] S.R.C., *Romana,* 9 maii 1893—*Fontes,* n. 6226.

[37] Feije, *De Nuptiarum Benedictione* (Amstelodami, 1848), Caput I, *De duplici nuptiarum benedictione,* § II, *De sensu formulae Ego vos coniungo, etc.,* pp. 9-64; e.g., p. 14: "Nos quoque cum cl. adversario formulae nostrae tribuimus hanc significationem, qua declaretur junctos esse sponsos in nomine Patris et Filii et Spiritus Sancti. Sed non est formula conjunctionis coram Deo, jam enim juncti sunt coram Deo per mutuum consensum. Est itaque formula conjunctionis, ut ait Binterim, in facie Ecclesiae, conjunctionis coram Ecclesia, coram foro externo,

that, over and above the solemn Nuptial Blessing of the Mass, there also existed, from the early centuries, a formula of simple blessing distinct from the solemn blessing. He admits that our present Ritual formula dates only from the 13th or 14th century, and shows how it evolved from the ancient formula, *"Deus Abraham, Deus Isaac, et Deus Jacob ipse vos conjungat, impleatque benedictionem suam in vobis,"* with which the priest blessed the married couple after they had exchanged their consent.[38]

"Therefore," he concludes, "there existed even in ancient times a double marriage blessing, the first of which was common to every marriage contracted between Catholics. This was given, after the marriage was contracted *per verba de praesenti,* at the doors of the Church as a rule, very rarely in the church itself. Later on, however, it was always imparted in church. The second was the solemn blessing which was sometimes called simply *benedictio,* since it was the marriage blessing *par excellence.* This was not given at second marriages."

If to the words of Feije is added, "nor was it given during the forbidden times," a transition is made to the following chapter of this dissertation which treats of the time for the celebration of marriage. The other point alluded to by Feije, namely, the place for the celebration of marriage, will be treated in the third chapter.

quod spectat publicitatem. Ratificat enim Ecclesia initum matrimonium, ut Ecclesiae mos habet, benedicendo, neque est simplex declaratio conjunctionis factae, sed quae fit *in nomine Patris et Filii et Spiritus Sancti,* seu cum signo benedictionis. Formula igitur haec rectissime dicitur formula *benedictionis* vel ex hoc solo capite; ulterius autem liquebit benedictionis sensum eam habere in mente Ecclesiae et auctorum."

[38] *Op. cit.,* Cap. I, § III, *Duplex semper in Ecclesia exstitit nuptiarum benedictio,* pp. 64-110. Feije admits that the distinction between the two blessings became clearer on the occasion of the theological discussions concerning the minister of Matrimony, on the occasion of the Council of Trent's legislation regarding the forbidden times for the solemnizing of marriage, and also on the occasion of a recognition of the growing frequency of mixed marriages. He contends however that the distinction always existed. As a positive proof of the existence of a double blessing he offers the *ordines* of Martene ranging from the tenth century onwards. Cf. Martene, *De Antiquis Ecclesiae Ritibus,* II, 615-663, for the texts of these *ordines.*

Chapter II

THE TIME FOR THE CELEBRATION OF MARRIAGE

Article I—Introduction

The purpose of this chapter is to consider the history of legislation in regard to the forbidden times for the solemnization of marriage *(tempus clausum, tempus feriatum),* from the early ages of the Church up to and including the Council of Trent. Since the Tridentine legislation remained in force till the Code, such a treatment, combined with an interpretation of the conciliar law of Trent as found in the works of pre-Code authors, will give an adequate conspectus of the historical development of the institute of forbidden times, and so prepare the way for a consideration in the second part of this work of the legislation contained in canon 1108 of the Code of Canon Law.

Before the historical question is treated directly, it will be useful to give a summary of the reasons underlying legislation on the forbidden times. Although according to divine law there are no days of the ecclesiastical year which are an obstacle to the valid and lawful celebration of marriage, the Church, however, from the early centuries, has wisely forbidden marriage, or at least its solemnities, during certain periods of the year, which were assigned as penitential seasons. That the faithful might give themselves more fully to prayer and penance, the celebration of marriage was forbidden as being ill-suited to the spirit of the season, because of the festivities and rejoicing which usually accompanied it.[1]

St. Robert Bellarmin gives an added reason for the prohibition, namely, that certain seasons are a preparation for the reception of

[1] Conc. Senon. (a. 1485): "Cum certis anni temporibus matrimonia ab ecclesia prohibeantur celebrari . . . et quia tunc omnes magis quam aliis temporibus debent devotioni et orationi intendere, a quibus tamen retrhait plurimum carnale commercium; eo etiam quod illis devotionis temporibus festa, choreae, ludi et convivia, quae in nuptiis fieri solent, non bene congruunt, sed verius opponuntur devotioni et contemplationi."—*Mansi,* XXXII, 429.

Holy Communion on the great feasts, i.e., Christmas, Easter and Pentecost. He adds that a probable reason for the reduction by the Council of Trent of the forbidden times from three periods to two, was that general Communion for all the faithful was rare on Pentecost, while it was the common practice at Easter and Christmas.[2]

Sanchez,[3] alluding to the errors of Chemnitz and Calvin says the former rejected the law of forbidden times as no longer useful, because the purpose of the law had ceased since Communion was of precept only during the Easter time; while the latter ridiculed the Church's law in regard to the closed times as a superstition tyrannically imposed by the Church.[4]

Chemnitz is refuted by the various motives alluded to above, which induced the Church to institute the forbidden times. The Church, in the Council of Trent, condemns Calvin's error, anathematizing anyone who says her prohibition is superstitious.[5]

These preliminary notions having been given as to the reasons for forbidden times, the actual legislation concerning forbidden times will now be traced from the early ages of the Church.

Article II—From the Earliest Times to the *Decretum Gratiani*

In the first three centuries there was no written law forbidding marriage or its solemnities at certain times of the year. Schulte

[2] *Disputationum Roberti Bellarmini Politani S.J., De Controversiis Christianae Fidei Tomi Quattuor* (4 vols., Neapoli, 1856), III, 857.

[3] *Disputationum de Sancto Matrimonii Sacramento Tomi Tres* (in 1 vol., Antverpiae, 1626), Liber VII., disp., 7, n. 1. Hereafter this work will be cited as *De Matrimonio*.

[4] Calvin, *Inst. Christ.*, 1 IV, C. XX, *in fine:* "Leges sanxerunt quibus tyrannidem suam firmarunt sed partim in Deum manifeste impias, partim in homines iniquissimas . . . Ne a Septuagesima ad octavas Paschae, tribus hebdomadibus ante natalem Joannis, ab Adventu ad Epiphaniam nuptiae celebrentur." Quoted by Esmein, *Le Mariage,* II, 321, note 1.

[5] Sess. XXIV, *De Sacramento Matrimonii,* can. XI. The text of this canon will be given later in its proper place in the historical development.

explains this by saying that in the first centuries it was unnecessary for the Church to make specific regulations on this point because of the fervent spirit and the strict customs of the first Christians.[6]

The first legislation in this regard is found in the Council of Laodicea in Phrygia, around the middle of the fourth century. The precise date of this council is a matter of dispute. The council enacted that neither the festivals of martyrs or marriages should be celebrated during Lent.[7]

Gratian has a canon which he ascribes to the Council of Lérida, held in 524 in the ecclesiastical province of Tarragona in Spain.[8]

This canon introduces a different use from that of Laodicea, viz., to Lent are added the season of Advent and also three weeks before the feast of St. John the Baptist. The genuine character of this canon, however, is highly doubtful.[9]

[6] Schulte, *Handbuch des Katholischen Eherechts* (Giessen, 1855), p. 316.

[7] C. 52: "Quod non oporteat in quadragesima nuptias vel natalitia celebrari."—Mansi, II, 572. Martin of Braga, in the sixth century, received this canon into his collection (*Capitula collecta a Martino Episcopo,* cap. XLVIII—Mansi, IX, 855). It is also found in Burchard of Worms (*Decret.* XIII, c. 10), and Ivo (*Decret.* VIII, c. 49), and was finally incorporated into the *Decretum Gratiani* (c. 8, 9, C. XXXIII, q. 4).

[8] C. 10, C. XXXIII, q. 4: "Quod non oporteat a septuagesima usque in octavas Paschae et tribus hebdomadibus ante festivitatem S. Joannis Baptistae et ab Adventu Domini usque post epiphaniam, nuptias celebrare: quod si factum fuerit separentur." This canon is given by Mansi under the heading *Fragmenta ex Concilio Ilerdensi* and is placed after the 16 canons of this council usually found in the old collections. Cf. Mansi, VIII, 616.

[9] Cf. Schulte, *Handbuch des Katholischen Eherechts,* p. 317; Wernz, *Ius Matrimoniale,* n. 544. The first collection to quote this canon was that of Burchard (*Decr.* IX, 4), wherefrom it passed directly or indirectly to Gratian. Burchard's custom to present secular laws, by false inscriptions, as canons of the Church is well known. For this particular canon Berardi (*Gratiani Canones,* I, 265) points to a Frankish Capitulary as the source. This capitulary prescribes three seasons of fast of forty days each before Christmas, Lent and after Advent. Cf. *MGH, Leges,* II, Tom. II, 82. This, says Berardi, with one of the several prohibitions against the use of marriage during seasons of fast, was combined into one canon by Burchard and ascribed to Lérida. Wernz's contention that it is a corruption of canon three of the Council of Seligenstadt

At any rate, from the evidence available, it seems that the law of the Council of Laodicea was the only one followed for the first ten centuries. And we see Pope Nicholas repeating the same prescription in his reply to the Bulgarian Christians.[10]

After the tenth century different customs regarding forbidden times prevailed in different localities. An example is the law of the Council of Selingenstadt (1022) made under the influence of Burchard, Bishop of Worms, who was at the Council. The Council in canon I gives a list of fast days: fourteen days before the feast of St. John the Baptist, before Christmas *(sic)*, the vigil of the Epiphany, the vigil of the Feast of the Holy Apostles, the vigil of the Assumption, the vigil of St. Lawrence and the vigil of All Saints. Then in canon III the council forbids marriage during Advent and until the octave of the Epiphany, from Septuagesima until the octave of Easter, and also "on the above mentioned fourteen days before the feast of St. John the Baptist, and on the above named fast days, and on the eve of all great feasts." [11]

The custom of the Roman church must have changed since the time of Nicholas I (858-867) for we find the Council of Benevento, held under Urban II (1088-1099) giving the forbidden times as follows: from Septuagesima until the octave of Easter, from the First Sunday of Advent until the octave of the Epiphany.[12]

The legislation concerning the forbidden times, incorporated by Gratian into his Decretum is contained in four canons of the

(1022) is not valid, since the canon is found in Burchard's collection which was compiled around the year 1012. Cf. Van Hove, *Commentarium Lovaniense,* Vol. I, Tom. I *Prolegomena* (Mechlinae, Romae: Dessain, 1928), 265.

[10] "Nec uxorem ducere, nec convivia facere in quadragesimali tempore convenire posse nullo modo arbitror."—Mansi, XV, 419. This law of Pope Nicholas is found in Gratian, c. 11, C. XXXIII, q. 4.

[11] C. 1, 3, Conc. Salegunstad.—Hartzheim, *Concilia Germaniae* (11 vols., Coloniae Augustae Agrippinensium, 1759-1790), III, 56. Hereafter this collection will be quoted as Hartzheim.

[12] Conc. Benevent. (1091), c. 4—Mansi, XX, 739.

fourth question in the thirty-third *causa.*[13] Canon eight repeats the legislation of Laodicea which gives Lent as the forbidden time. Canon nine also mentions only the season of Lent. It is ascribed by Gratian to the *Concilium Martini Papae* but in reality is from the collection of canons made by Bishop Martin of Braga in the sixth century.[14] Canon nine gives the very doubtful canon of Lérida already discussed which established the forbidden times from Septuagesima till the octave of Easter, three weeks before the feast of St. John, from Advent till after Epiphany. Canon ten mentions Lent as the forbidden time and incorporates the reply of Pope Nicholas to the Bulgarians.

Article III—From the *Decretum Gratiani* to the Council of Trent

Clement III (1187-1191), on the occasion of a reply to a doubt proposed by a certain bishop, gives a decision regarding the forbidden times. This letter of the Pope was incorporated into the authentic collection of Gregory IX in 1234,[15] and thus a more uniform law was established.

The doubt proposed by the bishop is concerned with the time mentioned in canon nine of the *Decretum,*[16] namely, the three weeks before the Feast of St. John. He inquires as to which of two opinions he is to follow: 1. that these three weeks are to be un-

[13] Causa XXXIII, q. 4:
c. 8: "Non oportet in Quadragesima aut nuptias vel quaelibet natalicia celebrari.
c. 9: "Non licet in Quadragesima natales martyrum celebrare . . . nec nuptias liceat in Quadragesima celebrari."
c. 10: "Non oportet a Septuagesima usque in octavam Paschae et tribus hebdomadibus ante festivitatem Sancti Joannis et ab Adventu Domini usque post Epiphaniam nuptias celebrare."
c. 11: "Nec uxorem ducere, nec convivia facere in quadragesimali tempore convenire posse ullo modo arbitror."

[14] *Capitula Collecta a Martino Episcopo Bracarensi.* Cap. XLVIII: "Non licet in Quadragesima natales martyrum celebrare, . . . sed nec natalitia neque nuptias liceat in quadragesima celebrare." Manis, IX—855.

[15] C. 4, X, *de feriis,* II, 9—Jaffé, 1659.

[16] C. 9, C. XXXIII, q. 4.

derstood as immediately preceding the Feast of St. John; or, 2. that they are to be understood in connection with the Feast of Pentecost, so that they are to be computed from Rogation Monday before Ascension Thursday until the Monday after the octave of Pentecost. The Pope replies that the latter opinion is the true one. Wernz points out that in this letter the Pope authentically defines the controversy regarding the computation of these days.[17]

So much is clear, but some parts of the letter are obscure. First of all, the letter seems to contradict itself. In one part the Pope says that nuptials cannot be celebrated from Septuagesima till seven days after Pentecost. In another section he seems to indicate that the time runs from Septuagesima till the octave of Easter, and then (after an interval of open times) from Rogation Monday till seven days after Pentecost. The *Abbas Panormitanus* gives several possible explanations. 1. That the Pope meant to exclude the time from Low Sunday till Rogation Monday in his general statement that marriages were forbidden from Septuagesima till seven days after Pentecost. 2. That the custom of the Roman church is to have the forbidden times from Septuagesima till the octave of Pentecost without interruption, while the canons of Gratian and the custom of other churches give the other computation, i.e., from Septuagesima till Low Sunday, and then for the three weeks before the Feast of St. John in the sense interpreted by the Pope.[18]

Then there is a dispute as to the meaning of the Pope's words when he says it has been the custom of the Roman church, in use for many years, that marriage can be contracted any time of the year. Some said that the Pope meant that marriage contracted during forbidden times, even without solemnity, would be illicit, though valid. This is contradicted by the Abbas Panormitanus[19] and Hostiensis.[20] These said that marriage could be contracted

[17] *Ius Matrimoniale,* n. 544, p. 419, note 2.

[18] *Abbatis Panormitani Commentaria in V Libros Decretalium* (5 vols. in 7, Venetiis, 1588), ad. c. 4, X, *de feriis,* II, 9, s. v. *Quia ergo.*

[19] *Loc. cit.*

[20] *Henrici de Segusio Cardinalis in V. Libros Decretalium Commentaria* (5 vols. in 3, Venetiis, 1581), ad c. 4, X, *de feriis,* II, 9, s. v. *Contrahautur.*

lawfully at any time of the year, but that solemnities, banquets, the *traductio in domum,* and the consummation of marriage were forbidden.

To sum up the legislation incorporated into the Decree of Gratian, and the interpretation given to it by the authentic collection of Gregory IX, the forbidden times for this period are as follows: From the First Sunday of Advent till the Feast of the Epiphany (according to some interpretations to the octave of the Epiphany) inclusively, from Septuagesima Sunday till Low Sunday inclusively, from Rogation Monday till Trinity Sunday inclusively.[21] During these times marriage could be contracted but solemnities, banquets, the *traductio in domum,* and the consummation of marriage were forbidden. This remained the general law till the Council of Trent.

We find these times repeated by provincial synods although at times there are variations. Most of these synods forbade only the solemn celebration of marriage. It will be useful to examine the legislation of these synods from the time of the Decretals to the Council of Trent, to observe their agreement with or discrepancy from the law of the Decretals.

A variation from the times of the general law is shown in the Synod of Bamberg held in 1491. The Lent and Advent periods are the same as the general law, but the period from Ascension is extended till the octave of Corpus Christi (instead of to Trinity Sunday). There is also a fourth period added, namely, the week during which the Feast of St. Mark and the Greater Litanies occur.[22] This same variation is found in the Synodal Statutes of the Diocese of Ratisbon in the year 1512.[23] The Constitution issued by Cardinal Campeggio, legate *a latere,* in the year 1524, at Ratisbon, makes a radical change in the forbidden times. It specifies that during the season of Lent, the last week of Advent, on the Feasts of Easter, Pentecost, and Christmas, and their

[21] Note however that the Feast of the Most Holy Trinity was not celebrated by the Roman Church at the time in question.

[22] Conc. Bamberg., Tit. XI—Hartzheim, V, 621.

[23] *Statuta Synodalia a Joanne Episcopo Ratisboniensi edita*—Hartzheim, VI,-103.

octave, during the Rogation Days, marriage cannot be solemnized.[24]

Other councils, over and above the general law, lay down a sanction for its violation. Thus the Synod of Utrecht, in the year 1293, places an excommunication on the spouses who violate the law of forbidden times and also on their retinue. This is repeated in the Synod of 1310.[25] The same penalty is stated by the Council of Benevento, in the year 1331, and is also applied to the pastor who celebrates the Nuptial Mass and imparts the Nuptial Blessing during these times.[26] Excommunication also is decreed against those who solemnize marriage in the forbidden times, by councils held in Paris in the years 1429 and 1485. The councils state that the forbidden solemnities include banquets, feasting, dancing or similar things. The penalty affects all who participate in such solemnities.[27] Penalties of excommunication against violators of forbidden times are found in the Council of Toledo in 1473[28] and the Synod of Bamberg in 1491.[29] The Statutes of the Diocese of Ratisbon in 1512 provide a penalty of suspension from office and benefice for parish priests who perform the solemnities of marriage.[30] A penalty of suspension from office is found also in the Council of Cologne in the year 1549.[31]

Although the law of forbidden times was strictly observed, in some councils one finds provision made for a dispensation from it

[24] *Constitutio ad Removendos Abusus*—Mansi, XXXII, 1089.

[25] Synodus Ultraject. (1293), c. XVIII—Hartzheim, IV, 18; Synodus Ultraject. (1310), c. XXVI—Hartzheim, IV, 172.

[26] Conc. Benevent., Cap. LI—Mansi, XXV, 963

[27] Conc. Senon.,—Mansi, XXVIII, 1112 and XXXII, 429. These councils are also called Councils of Paris because they were held there with the Bishop of Paris presiding. Although Sens was the metropolitan see, by the fifteenth century it had lost its former preeminence, and Paris, for all practical purposes was the metropolitan see, and its bishop overshadowed the archbishop of Sens.

[28] Conc. Tolet., C. XVI—Mansi, XXXII, 395. This council also mentions a fine for the priest who celebrates the Nuptial Mass.

[29] Conc. Bamberg. Tit. XI—Hartzheim, V, 621.

[30] *Statuta Synodalia*—Hartzheim, VI, 103.

[31] Conc. Colon.—Hartzheim, VI, 532.

to permit the Nuptial Mass and Blessing during these times.[32]

It has been shown that the general law of the time of the Decretals regarding forbidden times was followed in many local councils. It is true, however, that some variations occurred in regard to the times themselves, and also by reason of a penalty for violation, added over and above the prescription of the general law. In the following article the legislation of the Council of Trent will be considered. The Council restricted the times in use till then, but permitted any laudable and ancient customs in the matter of the forbidden times, to be retained.

Article IV—From the Council of Trent to the Code

A—The Conciliar Law of Trent

The Council of Trent, after having vindicated the canonical institute of forbidden times against the attacks of the reformers who claimed it was a superstitious practice,[33] restricted the general law of the Decretals. Henceforth the only forbidden times enjoined by general law are two: 1. from the first Sunday of Advent till the Feast of the Epiphany; 2. from Ash Wednesday till Low Sunday.[34] Both the first and last days of these prohibited periods are also included in the prohibition, as is evident from the word *inclusive* used by the Council. Sanchez shows that the word refers

[32] E.g. Synodus Ultraject.—Hartzheim, IV-18; Synodus Bamberg.—Hartzheim, V-621; Conc. Colon.—Hartzheim, VI-532; Conc. Salisburg.—Hartzheim, VI-529; Conc. Prov. Narbon.—Hardouin [*Acta Conciliorum et Epistolea, Decretales Constitutiones Summorum Pontificum* (12 vols., Parisiis, 1715)], X, 461. Hereafter this collection will be cited as Hardouin.

[33] Sess. XXVI *De Sacramento Matrimonii*, can. XI: "Si quis dixerit prohibitionem sollemnitatis nuptiarum certis anni temporibus superstitionem esse tyrannicam ab ethnicorum superstitione profectam; aut benedictiones et alias caeremonias, quibus ecclesia in illis utitur, damnaverit; anathema sit."

[34] Sess. XXIV, *de ref. matrim.*, C. X: "Ab Adventu Domini nostri Jesu Christi usque in diem Epiphaniae, et a feria quarta Cinerum usque in octavam Paschatis inclusive, antiquas sollemnium nuptiarum prohibitiones diligenter ab omnibus observari sancta synodus praecepit; in aliis vero temporibus nuptias sollemniter celebrari permittit, quas episcopi, ut ea qua decet modestia fiant curabunt. Sancta enim res est matrimonium, et sancte tractanda."

to *Epiphaniae* as well as to *ocvtavam Paschatis.*[35] The prohibition commenced at midnight of the first day of the forbidden season, and ended at midnight of the last day of the period.[36]

The general law regarding forbidden times as laid down by the Council of Trent was incorporated into the decrees of many local councils.[37] The Council of Trent, however, allowed any laudable customs or ceremonies of particular dioceses to be retained in the matter of Matrimony, providing such customs and ceremonies were over and above what the Council prescribed, and were not in direct contradiction to the Council's law. In fact the Fathers of Trent desired that these local customs should be retained.[38] Thus if a particular diocese wished to keep its ancient customs regarding forbidden times it could do so. An example is found in the legislation of the Synod of Worms held in the year 1610.[39] Among

[35] *De Matrimonio,* Lib., VII, disp. 7, n. 1.

[36] Sanchez held (*ibid.,* n. 2) that the Advent period started with first vespers of the preceding Saturday, since the office of Advent began then. This opinion, however, was contradicted by most pre-Code authors, e.g., Wernz, *Ius Matrimoniale,* n. 546; Schmalzgrueber, *Ius Ecclesiasticum Universum* (12 vols., Romae, 1845), Liber IV Decret. Tit. XVI, n. 30 (hereafter *Ius Eccles. Univ.*); Gasparri, *De Matrimonio* (ed. 1904), n. 1247.

[37] E.g., Conc. Remen. (1564)—Hardouin, X, 472; Conc. Mediolan. (1565)—Mansi, XXXIV-A, 72; Conc. Benevent. (1571)—Mansi, XXXVI-bis, 17; Conc. Rotomag. (1581)—Hardouin, X, 1221; Conc. Burdigal. (1583) Hardouin, X, 1351; Conc. Mediolan. (1573)—Mansi, XXXIV-A, 168; Conc. Mediolan (1579)—Mansi XXXIV-A, 481; *Statua Synodi Buscodensis* (1612)—Hartzheim, IX, 221.

[38] Sess. XXIV, *de ref. matrim.,* C. I. (circa finem): "Si quae provinciae aliis ultra praedictas laudabilibus consuetudinibus et caeremoniis hac in re utuntur, eas omnio retineri sancta synodus vehementer expotat."

[39] "Et quamvis ab Adventu Domini nostri usque in diem Epiphaniae et a feria IV cinerum usque ad octavam Paschae inclusive, antiquas sollemnium nuptiarum prohibitiones, diligenter ab omnibus observari Tridentinum Concilium praecipit; in aliis vero nuptias solemniter celebrari permittit: Nos nihil-ominus vestigiis antecessorum nostrorum ambulantes, statutum ipsorum de nuptiis, a die etiam Rogationum, usque ad festum Sanctissimae Trinitatis inclusive non celebrandis, juxta antiquam et laudabilem consuetudinem dioecesis hujus ratificandum esse duximus."—Hartzheim, IX, 124.

these laudable customs is also the practice which certain dioceses had of forbidding the solemnities of marriage on days of fast and abstinence.[40] Another custom which the Council permitted to be retained was the prohibition, during the forbidden times, not only of the solemnizing of marriage, but also of the marriage contract itself. This custom will be discussed when the interpretation and application of the law of the Council of Trent is considered.

So far the actual legislation of the Council of Trent has been considered. However, in the interpretation and application of this law not a few doubts arose, and the approved authors were divided on some points. A consideration of the law and its application and interpretation by the authors and the Sacred Congregations will give an adequate historical conspectus of the forbidden times from their restriction by the Council of Trent to their still further restriction by the Code of Canon Law.

B—*Interpretation and Application of the Law of the Council of Trent*

1—The Nature of the Impediment of Forbidden Times

The impediment of forbidden times *(impedimentum temporis clause)* of the Council was a prohibitive impediment not a diriment one. In fact it seems most probable that it never was a diriment impediment even from the beginning. Gasparri notes that some thought that in the ancient discipline of the church it was a diriment impediment.[41] They based their opinion, he says, on the authority of St. Peter Damian[42] and the canon in Gratian ascribed

[40] Cf. Conc. Prov. Strigon. (1858)—*Collectio Lacensis. Acta et Decreta Conciliorum Recentiorum,* (7 vols. Friburgi Briscoviae, 1870-1890), V, 25; Conc. Pragen. (1860)—*Coll. Lac.*, V, 519. This collection will be cited in this manner henceforth.

[41] *De Matrimonio* (ed. 1904), n. 1249; see also Wernz, *Ius Matrimoniale,* n. 544, p. 419, note 11.

[42] Opusculum XLI, *De tempore celebrandi nuptias,* cap. 4: "Censura canonica nuptias illicitis temporibus institutas remoto omni scrupulo dividit . . . Dicite inquam mihi . . . si in solo concubitu nuptiae constare dicendae sunt cur nuptiae contra legum mandata contractae usque ad

to the Council of Lérida.[43] This canon says that if the law forbidding the celebration of marriages is violated, the spouses are to be separated. Gasparri says that scholars, however, understand these words of St. Peter Damian and of Gratian's canon as referring to the separation of the spouses during the forbidden time only.[44] At any rate, as Gasparri says, marriage entered into in the forbidden times was always valid.[45] The question to be considered now is whether it was licit to enter into marriage, even without solemnities, during forbidden times. This question will be considered in the light of the legislation of particular diocesan and provincial laws, and in the light of the general law of the Church.

2—Particular Law and the Prohibition of the Marriage Contract

Since the Council of Trent desired any laudable customs or ceremonies, in the matter of marriage, to be retained, it is evident that it would not be contrary to the general law of the Council if certain dioceses, by custom or law, forbade, during the forbidden times, not only the solemnities of marriage, but even the marriage contract itself. That such particular customs or laws did exist is evident from the writers before the Code. Gasparri said that such a prohibition existed nearly everywhere *(fere ubique)*.[46]

divortium condemnantur." *MPL,* CXLV, 664. Benedict XIV in his *Institutiones Ecclesiasticae* (3 vols., Lovanii, 1762) notes that Christianus Lupus held the view that the impediment was a diriment one. Cf. *Instit. Eccle.*, Inst. LXXX, 19. This work will be cited in this manner henceforth.

[43] C. 10, C. XXXIII, q. 4.

[44] Cf. Glossa v. *Hinc etiam* ad dictum Grat. ante c. 8, C. XXXIII, q. 4: "Hic agit de illo impedimento quod dicitur tempus feriarum, de quo dicunt quidam quod impedit contrahendum et dirimat jam contractum quia contrahitur contra consuetudinem Ecclesiae . . . Alii melius discunt quod licet impediat non tamen dirimit."

[45] *De Matrimonio,* n. 1249.

[46] *De Matrimonio* (ed. 1904), n. 1250. Wernz (*Ius Matrimoniale,* n. 548) testifies to the existence of such a prohibition in many dioceses of France, Austria, and Belgium. Schmalzgrueber (*Ius Eccl. Univ.,* Lib. IV Decret., Tit. XVI, n. 34) and Reiffenstuel (*Ius Eccl. Univ.,* Lib. IV

In the places where such a law or custom existed it was unlawful for the marriage contract to be entered into during the *tempus clausum,* or for the simple blessing of the Ritual to be imparted. For the pastor to assist at the marriage he had to have the permission of the bishop, unless it were a case of urgent necessity.[47] The matter of the dispensation from such a particular law will be treated later.

The particular law or custom forbidding the marriage contract during the *tempus clausum* was upheld by the Holy See in several responses of the Sacred Congregations.[48]

Therefore in all dioceses where such a custom or law existed the pastor was obliged to follow it, and to obtain permission in each case, when marriage was to be contracted in the forbidden seasons.

3—The General Law and the Prohibition of Marriage Contract

Having seen that the marriage contract itself was often interdicted by particular law or custom, it remains to be seen whether the general law was equally stringent. Did the Council of Trent, besides forbidding the solemnities of marriage during the *tempus feriatum,* forbid also the contract of marriage itself? By general law was the bishop's permission necessary to enter licitly into the marriage contract, and to receive the blessing of the Ritual? Some authors, such as Barbosa,[49] Monacelli,[50] and Baruffaldo,[51] answer in the affirmative.

The reasons alleged by authors who hold this opinion are sum-

Decret., Tit. XVI, n. 13) attest its existence in many dioceses of Germany. Benedict XIV, says such a custom was of long standing in the diocese of Bologna. Cf. *Instit. Eccl.,* Inst. LXXX, 15.

47 Cf. Schmalzgrueber, *Ius Eccl. Univ.,* Lib. IV Decret., Tit. XVI, n. 134.

48 S. C. de Prop. Fide (C. P. pro Sin.-Tunkin Occident.), 21 iul. 1841—*Fontes,* n. 4791 S.R.C. *Montis Albani,* 14 aug. 1858—*Fontes,* n. 3079; S.R.C. *Mexicana,* 25 sept. 1875—*Fontes,* n. 6080.

49 Barbosa, *De officio et potestate episcopi* (Lugduni, 1666), Pars II, Alleg. XXXII, n. 194.

50 Monacelli, F., *Formularium Fori Ecclesiastici* (3 vols., Romae, 1844), Vol. I, p. 255.

51 Baruffaldo, G. *Ad Rituale Romanum Commentaria* (3 vols., Florentiae, 1817), Vol. I, p. 437.

marized by Sanchez [52] as follows: 1. Matrimony must be contracted *in facie Ecclesiae* and not clandestinely, but marriage *in facie Ecclesiae* is not permitted during these times, since the *benedictio nuptialis* is forbidden. 2. The canons of Gratian expressly forbid marriage during these times.[53] 3. Because the letter of Clement III *Capellanus tuus* is the first and only authoritative declaration that it is the custom of the Church that marriage can be contracted any time, but even this affirmation is limited later on in the letter by the statement that marriages are to be suspended during the forbidden times.[54]

This opinion seems to be favored by several responses of the Sacred Congregations. The Bishop of Montauban in France had asked whether the prohibition of forbidden times was to be understood only of the Nuptial Mass and the blessing contained therein, or also of the marriage itself celebrated with the form of the Ritual. The Congregation of Rites replied in the affirmative to the first part, and in the negative to the second, *provided the permission of the Bishop was obtained.* Another question of the bishop as to whether, in giving permission to contract marriage in forbidden times, he could also give permission for the Nuptial Mass and Blessing was answered in the negative.[55] This response might be explained by the fact that in many dioceses in France there was a local law forbidding even the marriage contract itself, were it not for another response of the same congregation to the Archbishop of Mexico. He asked if the response to the Bishop of Montauban was so general as to affect any diocese whatsoever, even where there was an immemorable custom to the contrary. The reply was in the affirmative and that such a custom was to be eradicated. To the further question as to whether the practice in the Archdiocese of Mexico, according to which parish priests were wont to perform marriages without solemnities during the forbidden times without asking permission of the Ordi-

[52] *De Matrimonio,* Lib. VII, disp. 7, n. 10.

[53] Cc. 8, 9, 10, 11, C. XXXIII, q. 4. For the texts cf. *supra,* p.

[54] C. 4, X, *de feriis,* II, 9.

[55] S.R.C. *Montis Albani,* 14 aug. 1858, ad I-II—*Fontes,* n. 5992.

nary, could be sustained, the answer was *negative* unless the Archbishop's permission had been obtained.[56]

A general decree of the same Congregation requires the bishop's permission for the simple celebration of marriage during forbidden times, thus implying that the general law of the Church forbids even the Ritual ceremonies and prayers during these times.[57]

In spite of these authorities and arguments there were many who denied that the general law of the Church forbade the marriage contract itself during the forbidden times, and who held, in consequence, that the Bishop's permission need not be asked to perform such a marriage. Gasparri says this opinion is the more probable one.[58]

This opinion is proved from the gloss preceding the canons of Gratian on forbidden times, which says that it is not forbidden to contract marriage in Lent.[59] The gloss also to the chapter of the Decretal *Capellanus tuus* is even more explicit, saying that only the solemnity of marriage is forbidden, and adding that the canons of Gratian must be interpreted in this way.[60]

This opinion is also sustained by the words of the Ritual which after stating that the solemnities of marriage are forbidden during

[56] S.R.C. *Mexicana,* 25 sept. 1875, ad I-II—*Fontes,* n. 6080.

[57] S.R.C., decr. gen. 30 iun. 1896, n. VI: "Temporibus vero prohibitis, nuptiae quidem celebrari possunt de licentia Episcopi; at sine sollemnitate, ideoque privatim; et omissa Missa et benedictione. Neque, iisdem temporibus, commemoratio pro Sponsis fieri potest in Missa occurente."—*Fontes,* n. 6265.

[58] *De Matrimonio* (ed. 1904), n. 1252. Some of the authors who held this opinion are: Sanchez, *De Matrimonio,* Lib. VII, disp. 7, n. 12; Schmalzgrueber, *Ius Eccl. Univ.,* Lib. IV Decret., Tit. XVI, n. 33; Reiffenstuel, *Ius Eccl. Univ.,* Lib., IV Decret., Tit. XVI, n. 12; Benedict XIV, *Instit. Eccl.,* Inst. LXXX, n. 2; St. Alphonsus, *Theologia Moralis . . . cura et studio P. L. Gaudé* (4 vols., 1905-1912), Tome IV, Lib. VI, n. 983.

[59] Glossa ad dictum Gratini *"Hinc etiam"* ante c. 8, C. XXXIII, qu. 4.

[60] Glossa ad c. 4 X *de feriis* II, 9: "quocunque tempore . . . et ita quolibet tempore potest matrimonium contrahi, sed nuptiarum sollemnitates tantum his diebus (ne carnaliter conjungantur) prohibentur, et secundum hoc intelligitur 33, qu. 4, c. 8 et c. seq."

certain times, adds that marriage can be contracted at any time of the year.[61]

The Sacred Congregation of the Council, also, in a number of responses declared that the marriage itself could be contracted at any time of the year.[62]

It may rightly be concluded with Gasparri that according to the general law of the Church, at least in the post-Tridentine period, there was no prohibition properly so called of the marriage contract itself during the *tempus clausum,* but only a counsel that marriage should not be contracted during these times, even without solemnities. Hence the canons of Gratian and the letter of Clement III may be understood as referring to the solemnities which are forbidden and not to the marriage itself; or they may be looked upon as laws which, in the period now being considered, had become obsolete. Therefore when the Congregation of Rites demanded the permission of the ordinary for the private celebration of marriage, it did so that the counsel mentioned above might be better observed. Gasparri says this permission was always granted at the insistence of the parties, since there was no strict prohibition of law.[63] As Sanchez wisely observes, such a strict prohibition of the marriage contract itself would be ill in accord with the wisdom and prudence of the church.[64]

4—The Extent of the Prohibition of the Council of Trent

It has been seen that, most probably, according to the general law of the Council of Trent, the marriage contract itself was not forbidden during the *tempus clausum,* but only the solemnities of marriage. The question now arises: what were these solemnities

[61] *Rituale Romanum Pauli V Pont. Max. jussu editum et a Benedicto XIV auctum et castigatum* (Ratisbonae, Romae, 1911), Tit. VII *De Sacramento Matrimonii,* n. 18: "Matrimonium autem omni tempore contrahi potest."

[62] S.C.C., *Arianen.,* mense maio 1587—*Fontes,* n. 2177; S.C.C., *Interamnen.,* 27 mart. 1591— *Fontes,* n. 2225; S.C.C., *Agrigentina,* 11 mai. 1599—*Fontes,* n. 2324; S.C.C. 20 iul. 1619—*Fontes,* n. 2415; S.C.C. *Bosnen.,* 2 dec. 1644—*Fontes,* n. 2654.

[63] *De Matrimonio,* (ed. 1904), n. 1252.

[64] *De Matrimonio,* Lib. VII, disp. 7, n. 12.

which were forbidden during the closed times? As Benedict XIV observed, the Council of Trent, while shortening the forbidden times, stated nothing new regarding what was forbidden during those times, but merely commanded that the ancient prohibitions of solemn nuptials should be observed by everyone.[65] What, then, according to the opinion of the canonists, were the *antiquae prohibitiones nuptiarum* which the Council of Trent commanded to be observed?

(a)—*Benedictio Nuptialis*

All canonists agreed that the Nuptial Blessing was forbidden by the general law. But in what precisely did the Nuptial Blessing consist? The Congregation of Rites said that it consisted of the prayers found in the votive mass *pro sponso et sponsa,* namely the prayer *"Propitiare, Domine,"* and the prayer *"Deus, qui potestate,"* to be said before the *Libera nos,* and the prayer *"Deus Abraham,"* to be said after the *Benedicamus Domino* or the *Ite Missa Est.*[66] This Mass and the prayers which constitute the Nuptial Blessing were forbidden during the closed time. The Sacred Congregations declared this in several responses.[67] Nor, during these times, could orations of the Mass *pro sponso et sponsa* and the Nuptial Blessing be added to the Mass of the day when, on account of the rubrics, the votive Mass is not permitted.[68] Neither could the Nuptial Blessing be separated from the Mass and given outside of Mass at any time.[69]

65 *Inst. Eccl.,* Inst. LXXX. n. 4.—Cf. the text of Sess. XXIV, *de ref. matrim,* c. X, *supra,* p. 21, note 34.

66 S.R.C. *Romana,* 9 maii 1893, ad III—*Fontes,* n. 6226.

67 S.C. de Prop. Fide (C.P. pro Sin.-Tunkin. Occident), 21 iul 1841, ad I—*Fontes,* n. 4791; S.C.S. Off., 31 aug. 1881—*Fontes,* n. 1071; S.R.C. *Limburgen.,* 23 iun. 1853, ad III—*Fontes,* n. 5967; S.R.C., decr. gen., 30 iun. 1896, n. VI—*Fontes,* n. 6265.

68 S.R.C., *Montis Pessulani,* 31 aug. 1839— *Fontes,* n. 5899; S.R.C., decr. gen. 30 iun. 1896, n. VI—*Fontes,* n. 6265

69 S.R.C., *Montis Pessulani,* 31 aug. 1839—*Fontes,* n. 5899; S.R.C,. *Limburgen,* 23 iun. 1853—*Fontes,* n. 5967; S.R.C., *Belemen de Para.,* 12 feb. 1909—*Fontes,* n. 6372. However an indult was granted by Pius IX to the Province of Quebec in 1865 permitting the nuptial blessing to be given outside of mass. Cf. *Coll. Lac.,* III-687.

However, the spouses who had been unable to receive the Nuptial Blessing because of the forbidden times, could receive it during the Nuptial Mass celebrated after the closed time had elapsed, although there was no obligation that they should request it.[70]

During the forbidden times, however, the blessing of the Ritual contained in the formula *Ego conjungo vos* could be given. These words, though containing a blessing,[71] are not the solemn Nuptial Blessing forbidden during the closed time.

After the ceremonies of the Ritual had been performed during forbidden times, the spouses, if they wished to receive Holy Communion, could assist at Mass, provided no Nuptial Blessing was given and no commemoration was made of the *missa pro sponso et sponsa.*[72]

As to the violation of the precept forbidding the imparting of the solemn blessing in forbidden times, the authors agreed that it was a serious sin for the pastor to give this blessing, and for the parties to receive it.[73] The pastor who violated this law was to be punished by the bishop. Since there was no penalty laid down by the law, the penalty was an arbitrary one to be inflicted at the discretion of the bishop. The parties were to be punished by being separated until after the forbidden times, unless there was danger of incontinence, which condition, Gasparri notes, would always be verified.[74] In this case some arbitrary penalty was to be imposed on them by the bishop.[75] The same penalties would apply if the diocesan law forbidding the marriage contract itself had been violated.[76]

There will follow later a discussion of the possibility of a dispensation from the prohibition of the solemn blessing during forbidden times.

[70] S.C.S. Off., 31 aug. 1881—*Fontes,* n. 1071; S.R.C., decr. gen., 30 iun. 1896, n. VI—*Fontes,* n. 6265.

[71] Cf. *supra,* p. 11.

[72] Cf. Benedict XIV, *Instit. Eccl.,* Inst. LXXX, nn. 8-11.

[73] Sanchez, *De Matrimonio,* Lib. VII, disp. 7, n. 3; Gasparri, *de Matrimonio* (ed. 1904), n. 1255.

[74] *De Matrimonio* (ed. 1904), n. 1259.

[75] Sanchez, *De Matrimonio,* Lib. VII, disp. 7, nn. 4-5.

[76] Gasparri, *op. cit.,* n. 1258.

(b) —*Convivia*

According to canon eleven of Gratian's canons on forbidden times wedding banquets were forbidden during Lent.[77] But as Gasparri observes this canon of Nicholas I was enacted at a time when the Lenten fast was very rigid. The wedding meal in later times had become a natural sequel to the marriage itself, and if everything was done in moderation there was no sin at all. If there was some excess not altogether in keeping with the time there would be a slight sin.[78] But as Sanchez says to constitute a serious sin there would have to be such an excess as to notably detract from the sanctity of the forbidden times, and such as to cause serious scandal.[79]

(c)—*Traductio in Domum*

The bringing of the bride to the husband's house, the *traductio in domum,* a custom which goes back even to Roman times, was one of the solemnities forbidden during the *tempus clausum.* This was usually done with much ceremony, the bridal cortege being accompanied by singers and musicians, followed by a wedding banquet at the bride's new home. The reason why such a solemnity would be forbidden is evident. Such excessive rejoicing was ill in accord with the spirit of the forbidden times.

Some authors held that any form of *traductio* was forbidden, even without the solemnities described above. They based their argument on the ruling of Pope Nicholas found in Gratian..[80] This they supported by the argument that the Council of Trent urged the spouses not to cohabit until they had received the priestly blessing, which could not be given during the forbidden times.[81] They further strengthened their argument by a number

[77] C. 11, C. XXXIII, q. 4: "Nec convivia facere in quadragesimali tempore . . ."

[78] Gasparri, *op. cit.,* n. 1259.

[79] *De Matrimonio,* disp. VII, Lib. 7, nn. 7, 18.

[80] C. 11, C. XXXIII, q. 4: "Nec *uxorem ducere,* nec convivia facere in quadragesimali tempore convenire posse nullo modo arbitror."

[81] Sess. XXIV, *de ref. matrim,* c. I: ". . . eadem sancta synodus hortatur ut conjuges ante benedictionem sacerdotalem in templo suscipiendam in eadem domo non cohabitent."

of responses of the Congregation of the Council, all of which repeat the phrase: *nuptiarum solemnia, convivia, traductio in domum, carnalisque copula* when naming the things forbidden during the closed time.[82] This opinion was sponsored by Fagnanus,[83] who also claimed that the consummation of marriage was forbidden. Gasparri admits that this opinion is probably more in accord with the ancient canons, but states that in more recent times authors make a distinction between the *traductio solemnis,* namely that which is accompanied by singing and other signs of rejoicing, and the *traductio privata,* which takes place without any merriment or rejoicing associated with the *traductio solemnis.*[84] In their view the *traductio solemnis* was forbidden but not the *traductio privata.* This Sanchez calls the truer opinion but even in the case of the *solemnis traductio* he can see no serious sin, unless things were carried to such an excess as to be altogether out of keeping with the forbidden times, and so cause scandal to the faithful.[85]

(d)—*Carnalis Copula*

As a logical consequence of his opinion concerning *traductio in domum* Fagnanus held that the use of marriage was forbidden to those who were married during the forbidden times. He claimed that his opinion was the common opinion of nearly all the canonists.[86] He offered in support of his opinion the responses of the Congregation of the Council cited above. He was opposed by Sanchez who says there is no prohibition of consummating marriage during the forbidden times.[87] He continues by saying that Fagnanus' argument that the copula is forbidden because the

[82] S.C.C., *Arianen.,* mense maio 1587—*Fontes,* n. 2177; S.C.C., *Interamen,* 27 mart. 1591—*Fontes,* n. 2225; S.C.C., *Agrigentina,* 11 maii 1599—*Fontes,* n. 2324; S.C.C., 20, iul, 1619—*Fontes,* n. 2415; S.C.C., *Bosnen.,* 2 dec. 1644—*Fontes,* n. 2654.

[83] Fagnani, *Commentaria in Secundum Librum Decretalium* (4 vols., Venetiis, 1697), II, in cap. IV, *de feriis "Capellanus,"* p. 88.

[84] *De Matrimonio* (ed. 1904), n. 1256.

[85] *De Matrimonio,* Lib., VII, disp. 7, nn. 16-18.

[86] *Op. cit.,* II, In cap. IV *de feriis*—p. 90.

[87] *De Matrimonio,* Lib. VII, disp. 7, n. 23.

traductio is forbidden, is not valid. The *traductio* is forbidden not to prevent the consummation of the marriage but to avoid the signs of excessive mirth and rejoicing which usually accompany the *traductio solemnis.* Benedict XIV supports Sanchez's opinion and says that a burden should not be imposed on the faithful, which is not clearly imposed on them by law.[88] Regarding the responses of the Congregation of the Council which were mentioned above, Benedict XIV says that it is uncertain whether they forbid only the *solemnis traductio* or also the *privata traductio,* and that it is also doubtful whether the spouses must abstain from the use of marriage only after the *solemnis traductio* or also after the *privata traductio.* At any rate it is certain that the same Congregation in another response permitted the *privata traductio* and hence the *coupla carnalis.*[89]

Regarding the wish of the Council of Trent that the spouses should not cohabit,[90] it should be noticed that these words were a counsel and not a command, since the Council used the word *hortatur.*

It can be concluded with Sanchez that the only act forbidden

[88] *Instit. Eccl., Inst.* LXXX, n. 19: "Illam tenendam reipsa ducimus, ne vinculum fidelibus injiciatur, quod a nulla lege clare praescribitur. Insuper id consuetudini, et instituto Ecclesiae valde consentaneum est, quae humanae fragilitatis gratia, rationeque habita, paulatim a veteri disciplina recessit, cum de re ejusmodi quaestiones inducerentur." Benedict (Inst. LXXX, n. 20) quotes Van Espen as holding the same opinion: "Quidquid sit de hac sententia Fagnani, attenta canonum antiquorum rigorosa expressione, hoc certum est hodie dictis temporibus nequaquam vetitum esse actum matrimonialem, sed ad summum consilii esse eis temporibus abstinere, ut mente elatiore, et a carnalibus voluptatibus magis libera vacent orationi, et pietatis exercitiis."

[89] S.C.C., 10, iun, 1684: "Nonnulli parochi pro sua et matrimonia contrahentium quiete supplicant declarari: An concessa per Episcopum licentia contrahendi matrimonium temporibus a S.C. in c. 10 Sess. 24 *de ref. mat.* vetitis in iis locis, in quibus dispositio ejusdem Concilii ad ipsum quoque matrimonii contractum reperitur a consuetudine extensa, dicatur etiam permissa traductio sponsae seu uxoris ad domum viri? Resp. Affirmative, dummodo traductio fiat absque solemnitatibus." —*Fontes,* n. 2880.

[90] C. I. *De ref. matrim.*

under pain of serious sin in these forbidden times was the solemn Nuptial Blessing.[91]

C—*Dispensation From the Conciliar Law of Trent*

There was no question that, if there was a particular law forbidding the marriage contract itself during the forbidden times, the bishop could dispense from the law and permit the marriage to take place with the formula and blessing of the Ritual. Since such a law was a particular one the bishop was competent to dispense. But the question arises: could the bishop dispense in the general law of the Church and permit the solemn Nuptial Blessing to be given during the forbidden times? Sanchez says the bishop ordinarily could not do so because a subordinate cannot dispense from a superior's law, but he admits that the bishop could dispense in a very urgent case when recourse to the Holy See was difficult.[92] But Sanchez' opinion is contradicted by Gasparri,[93] Feije,[94] and De Becker,[95] all of whom declare that the bishop can never permit the solemn blessing to be imparted. This power is also denied to the bishop in the responses of the Sacred Congregations.[96]

[91] *De Matrimonio,* Lib. VII, disp. 7, n. 18: "Solas nuptiarum benedictiones hoc tempore vetitas esse sub mortali existimo."

[92] *De Matrimonio,* Lib. VII, Disp., 7, n. 6.

[93] *De Matrimonio* (ed. 1904), n. 255: ". . . nec Episcopus id permittere ullo modo potest . . . Hinc errant Sanchez, Giovine, aliique."

[94] *De Imped. et Disp. Matr.* n. 613, p. 516, note 1: "Immerito igitur eam potestatem episcopo recentius attribuerunt Giovine t. 1, p. 686 sq. causam valdem gravem et urgentem requirens, et van de Burg, *De matr.,* n. 293, *De Disp.* n. 133."

[95] *De Sponsalibus et Matrimonio Praelectiones Canonicae* (Lovanii et New York, 1903), p. 260.

[96] S.R.C., *Linburgen.,* 23 iun. 1853 ad 3: "An Episcopus in Casibus particularibus et ob rationables et graves causas etiam in hoc dispensare possit ut secluso quidem semper alio quocumque appartatu ac strepitu, nuptiarum benedictio tamen sollemnis more debito adhibeatur? Resp. In casu nuptiae celebrentur sine sollemnitate ideoque privatim sine Missa et sine benedictione temporibus prohibitis."—*Fontes,* n. 5967. S.R.C. *Montis Albani,* 14 aug. 1858 ad II: "An facta per Episcopum licentia contrahendi Matrimonia temporibus a S. Concilio Tridentino vetitis,

The Roman Pontiff, then, was the only one who could dispense in this impediment of forbidden times and permit the Nuptial Blessing. But as De Becker observed,[97] generally there was no reason for the Pope to permit the solemn blessing, since the simple blessing permitted by the general law could always be given, and moreover the Nuptial Blessing could be imparted after the forbidden season had elapsed. However, for very special reasons the Pope sometimes granted indults for mission countries by virtue of which the Nuptial Blessing could be given even during the forbidden times.[98]

censeatur etiam permissa benedictio conjugum per preces et orationes in Missa pro Sponsis contentas? Et. quatenus negative: An possit Episcopus in casu eam facultatem concedere? Resp. Negative in omnibus." —*Fontes*, n. 5992.

[97] *Loc. cit.*

[98] S. C. de Prop. Fide. (C. P. pro Sin.—Vic. Ap. Sutchuen.) 31 iul. 1796—*Fontes*, n. 4649; S. C. de Prop. Fide (C. P. pro Sin.—Tunkin. Occident.) 21 iul. 1841—*Fontes*, n. 4791.

Chapter III

THE PLACE FOR THE CELEBRATION OF MARRIAGE

In Chapter I it was shown that from the early centuries the Church, recognizing the sacred character of the marriage contract, sanctified the celebration of matrimony by religious ceremonies and by the Nuptial Blessing. But although the Church desired that marriage be entered into with her intervention, and, as time went on, made laws forbidding its celebration without the offices of her minister, up to the Council of Trent she did not invalidate such unions, provided there was a valid consent and there was no diriment impediment. Throughout the Middle Ages, to combat the growing evil of clandestine marriages, she enjoined the public religious celebration of marriage under pain of grave ecclesiastical penalties. From this two-fold source, then, flows the development of legislation commanding that marriage should be contracted in the church: 1. the religious character of matrimony,—because, since it is a sacrament, it should be received in church which is the usual place for the reception of the sacraments;[1] 2. its social character—it is an indissoluble contract which has far reaching consequences on society and hence should not be entered into secretly and in such a manner as to be easily repudiated later.

Article I—From the Beginning to the Council of Trent

From the evidence offered in the first chapter showing the existence of the priestly blessing and of the Nuptial Mass, and from the writings of the Fathers and the civil legislation of the Frankish kings urging or commanding the reception of this blessing, the place for the celebration of marriage is indirectly indicated. For, if the Nuptial Mass as contained in the sacramentaries was celebrated and the Nuptial Blessing given, the ceremony would naturally take place in the church. But it is not until the time of

[1] II Conc. Mediolian (1569), c. 28: "Ne parochus ullo alio loco quam in ecclesia ipsa, quae sacramentorum proprius locus est, sponsos matrimonio jungat."—Mansi, XXXIVA, 114.

Benedict the Levite that explicit mention is made of the place of marriage. In his so-called Capitulary of Charlemagne and Louis the Pious it is stated that the marriage *(nuptiae)* must be celebrated in the church before the people. In the church the priest is to inquire if there exists consanguinity or a previous marriage; and if there is nothing to hinder the marriage, the bride is to be blessed with the blessing contained in the sacramentary.[2]

From the fifth century onwards the Church came into contact with the Germanic peoples. These, after their conversion, continued to adhere to their ancient customs, at least to those such as were not contrary to Christianity. Among most of these people marriage was usually entered into by the transfer of guardianship over the bride from the parents to her husband. This transfer was accompanied by certain ceremonies which constituted the *matrimonium legitimum.*[3] To these ceremonies were added the sacred rites of the Church and especially the priestly blessing. But since most of these ancient ceremonies could not conveniently be performed in the church, they took place before the doors of the church. Then, the newly wedded couple entered the church to assist at the Holy Sacrifice and receive Communion. This is the origin of the phrase in *facie Ecclesiae* or *in conspectu Ecclesiae* which first had the literal meaning of "at the doors of the church" and later came to signify a marriage contracted in accordance with the requirements enacted by the Church and (after the Council of Trent) according to the form prescribed by her. This phrase or its equivalent was used in the legislation of many councils and in the liturgical books, and from the alternate expressions used, for example, *ad valvas ecclesiae,* it is clear that it often signified the physical place of the marriage. As Villien observes, in many dioceses of France from the eleventh to the fifteenth centuries the

[2] Bened. Levit., *Capit. Lib. III,* c. 179 (*Pseudo-Capit. Karoli Magni et Ludov. Pii,* Lib. VIII)—*MGH. Leges,* II, tom II, p. 113. For the sources used in composing this canon see Seckel, "*Studien zu Benedictus Levita,*" VIII, 1,—*Neues Archiv der Gesellschaft für ältere deutsche Geschichtskunde, XXXIX* (1914), 393-398.

[3] For a fuller description of the Germanic marriage customs see Joyce, *Christian Marriage,* pp. 48-52; and Wernz, *Ius Matrimoniale,* n. 156.

exchange of consent took place at the church door.[4] Wernz says the custom of celebrating the marriage at the church door existed in France and England up to the sixteenth century.[5]

The *Ordines* collected by Martene attest to the fact that from the tenth to the sixteenth century, in France at least, the actual marriage ceremony took place at the doors of the church. After the exchange of consent, the blessing of the ring, and the imparting of the simple blessing, "*Deus Abraham, Deus Isaac, et Deus Jacob ipse vos conjungat, impleatque benedictionem suam in vobis,*" the spouses entered the church to assist at the marriage Mass (in France this was usually the votive Mass of the Most Holy Trinity), during which the solemn Nuptial Blessing was usually imparted, although sometimes it was not given until after Mass was over.[6]

While most of the *Ordines* of Martene point to the doors of the church as the place for the celebration of the actual marriage ceremony, nevertheless all are not in agreement on this point. Some of these *Ordines* say simply that the marriage is to be celebrated in church.[7] Others indicate both places and say that local custom is to be followed in the matter.[8] In this variance of custom regarding the place of marriage Villien sees the possible origin of the rubric of the Roman Ritual (which prescription remained in force till the Code), that though it is highly fitting that

[4] *History and Liturgy of the Sacraments,* p. 283.

[5] *Ius Matrimoniale,* n. 156.

[6] Martène, *De Antquis Ecclesiae Ritibus,* II, *Ordines* II-XV, pp. 616-663. The rubrics of the *Ordines* employ a variety of phrases to indicate the place where the marriage ceremony is performed. E.g. *Ordo* II (11th cent.): "*ante ostium Ecclesiae;*" Ordo III (12th cent.): "*ad januas ecclesiae;*" *Ordo* VIII (15th cent.): "*ad valvas ecclesiae;* " *Ordo* IX (undated): "*quando sunt ante ostium templi;*" *Ordo* X (15th Cent.): "*ante valvas ecclesiae;* "*Ordo* XIV (undated) says the marriage is to take place before the doors of the bride's parish church. It is interesting to note that *Ordo* XIII (undated) replaced the usual invocative form of the simple blessing, i.e., *Deus Abraham, etc.,*" by an indicative one, "*Despondo vos in facie Ecclesiae.*"

[7] E.g., *Ordo* V (14th cent.); *Ordo* VII (14th cent.).

[8] E.g., *Ordo* XII (undated); *Ordo* XV (undated).

marriage be celebrated in church, however, if it takes place in a private house in the presence of the parish priest and the witnesses, the newly wedded couple are to come to the church afterwards to receive the Nuptial Blessing. He says such an assumption is a justifiable one.[9]

The precise ruling that marriage should be contracted at the church door is also embodied in the legislation of local councils at least from the year 1200. The Council of London in 1200 uses the phrase *"in facie ecclesiae."* [10] While this could equally mean that the marriage must be contracted with the knowledge and offices of the Church without having any specific reference to the place, it is quite likely that the place also is indicated, namely in front of the church. Cronin points out that in pre-Reformation days in England the interchange of consent took place not in the church, but outside the church door, so that the marriage was contracted literally in *facie ecclesiae.*[11]

The Statutes of the diocese of Rouen expressly mention the doors of the church as the place of marriage and place a penalty

[9] *History and Liturgy of the Sacraments,* p. 283. Cf. also *Rituale Romanum Pauli V Jussu Editum et a Benedicto XIV Auctum et Castigatum* (Romae, 1911), Tit. VII, *De Sacramento Matrimonii,* c. I, n. 16: "Matrimonium in ecclesia maxime celebrari debet; sed si domi celebratum fuerit praesente Parocho et testibus, sponsi veniant ad ecclesiam benedictionem accepturi." This prescription, however, has been changed in the Ritual, which was revised in 1925 in order to bring it up to date with the Code. Cf. *Rituale Romanum Pauli V Jussu Editum . . . atque Auctoritate Sanctissimi D.N. Pii Papae XI ad Norman Codicis Juris Canonici Accomodatum* (4 ed. juxta typicam, Ratisbonae: Pustet, 1935), Tit. VII, *De Sacramento Matrimonii,* c. I, n. 20. The new Ritual repeats canon 1109 of the Code. Cf. *infra,* Chapter VII. Hereafter the former edition of the Ritual will be cited simply as *Rituale Romanum;* the new Ritual will be cited as *Rituale Romanum (ad normam Codicis).*

[10] C. XI: "Nec contrahatur aliquod matrimonium . . . nisi *publice in facie ecclesiae,* et praesente sacerdote; et si secus factum fuerit, non admittantur alicubi in ecclesia; nisi speciali auctoritate episcopi."—Mansi XXII, 719.

[11] *The New Matrimonial Legislation* (London, Glasgow, New York, 1909), p. 122, note. 1.

of excommunication on the violation of this statute.[12] The same prescription is found in the Synodical Statutes of the Church of Le Mans, and the penalty is incurred not only by the spouses but also by those who give aid or counsel in breaking the law.[13] This reference to the contracting of marriage at the doors of the church continues to be repeated in provincial councils at least up to the beginning of the fourteenth century and reappears occasionally later on.[14]

From the fourteenth century on there is hardly any reference to the church door, but the councils instead specify the church itself as the place for marriages, and often the parish church itself is specified. The Council of Sens (also called the Council of Paris) in 1429 gives the reasons for its prescription that marriage be celebrated publicly in the church, namely the dignity of the sacrament and the avoidance of scandal. The same council imposes a penalty on priests who perform marriages in private oratories without permission, and on bishops who grant this permission without urgent cause.[15] The prescription of this council was reenacted verbatim by the Council of Sens (Paris) in 1485.[16] The Council of Seville in 1512 expressly mentions the parish church as the place of marriage. Any priest who, without permis-

[12] *Praecepta Antiqua Dioecesis Rotomagensis* (1235), LXVI: "Prohibemus sub poena excommunicationis et magnae emendae, ne personae alique consentiant matrimonialiter per verba de praesenti, donec sint ante fores Ecclesiae, quando debet nuptials benedictio celebrari."—Mansi, XXIII, 383.

[13] *Statuta Synodalia Ecclesiae Cenomanensis* (1247)—Manis, XXIII, 748.

[14] Cf. Constitutiones Syndoales Valentinae Dioecesis (1255): ". . . *ad ostium ecclesiae*"—Mansi XXIII, 891; Conc. Langes. (1278): ". . . *ante portas ecclesiae*"—Mansi, XXIV, 213; Conc. Exon. (1287: ". . . *in ostio ecclesiae*"—Mansi, XXIV, 794; Synodus Baioc. (c. 1300): ". . . *ante fores ecclesiae.*"—Mansi, XXV, 72; Constitutiones Ricardi Poore Sarum Episcopi (c. 1217): ". . . *in facie ecclesiae praesenti sacerdote.*"—Mansi, XXII, 1125; Conc. Lugdun. (1449); ". . . *nisi intra fores ecclesiae*"—Mansi, XXXII, 97; Conc. Prov. Liman. (1592): ". . . *ceremoniae vero consuetae fiant ad ecclesiae januas.*"—Mansi, XXXVI-Bis, 207.

[15] C. IV—Mansi, XXVIII, 1111-1112.

[16] Mansi, XXXII, 428-429.

sion performs marriages elsewhere, is subjected to suspension for a year and a fine.[17] The Council of Cologne in 1536 decrees that the marriage should be performed in the church during Mass, and states that those who prefer private dwellings for the ceremony, in the words of St. Paul, despise the Church of God.[18] The Council of Augusburg (1548) states that marriages should be contracted only in the church, which is the proper place for the administration of the sacraments.[19] This reason is repeated after the Council of Trent by Cardinal Charles Borromeo in the synods of Milan.[20] The Council of Cologne in 1549 states that the marriage is to take place only in the church after the celebration of Mass at which the future spouses assist.[21] The Council of Narbonne in 1551 points to the parish church as the place for the reception of the sacrament of matrimony.[22]

Since marriages are to be performed publicly in the church, usually in the parish church, it is evident that all the councils which command this implicitly forbid marriages elsewhere, for example, in private houses, chapels, oratories, or exempt churches. In fact there is found in some councils an explicit prohibition against the use of such places for the marriage ceremony. For example, the Council of Canterbury in 1328 suspends from office for a year the priest who presumes to celebrate marriage anywhere but in the parish church or a chapel having parochial rights.[23] This is much more stringent than the Council of Exeter's prescription some fifty years earlier (1287), which merely required that the marriage be performed publicly and in any place

[17] C. XX—Mansi, XXXII, 601.

[18] Hardouin, IX, 2011.

[19] Hartzheim, VI, 359.

[20] Cf. *infra*, p. 46.

[21] Mansi, XXXII, 1397-a.

[22] Hardouin, X, 461.

[23] Wilkins, *Concilia Magnae Britanniae et Hiberniae* (4 vols., Londini, 1639-1664), II, 554. This collection will be cited hereafter as Wilkins.

in accord with the reverence due to the sacrament.[24] In Germany the Council of Magdeburg (1370) forbids anyone, even persons of high position, from contracting marriage in private houses or outside of the church.[25]

A Council of Lyons in 1449, after prescribing that marriage be contracted *"intra fores ecclesiae parochialis"* by the pastor of the parties or his assistant, states that those who contract marriage in chapels or exempt churches are to be excommunicated.[26]

It has been seen from the ancient *Ordines* collected by Martene and from a number of councils assembled in France, Germany and England that the custom existed in these countries, at least from the tenth century to the fourteenth or fifteenth century, of celebrating the marriage at the doors of the church, and that this ceremony was usually followed by the Nuptial Mass and Blessing in the church. As time went on the ancient custom seemed to be dying out and instead of the former phrases such as *ad ostium ecclesiae, ad valvas ecclesiae, etc.*, in their place the words *in ecclesia*, or *inecclesia parochiali* were used, and prescriptions are found forbidding marriages in private houses, chapels or exempt churches. It is true the phrase *in facie ecclesiae* still reappears in legislation, but it has lost its former material sense of the facade of the church, and comes to mean primarily a marriage celebrated with the juridical formalities required by the Church. This is the phrase canonized by the Council of Trent when it established a juridical form required for the validity of marriage. In the next article the period extending from the Council of Trent to the Code will be considered with a view to discovering whether there was any general law regarding the place of marriage. In this connection the particular legislation of local and provincial councils will also be considered.

[24] "Debet igitur hoc sacramentum cum discretione magna et reverentia celebrari in locis honestis, et tempore congruo, cum omni modestia et maturitate; non in tabernis, potationibus, et commensationibus, non secretis locis, latebris, et suspectis, ed palam et sobrie celebretur."—Wilkins, II, 135.

[25] Mansi, XXVII, 583.

[26] C. XIV—Mansi, XXXII, 97.

Article II—From the Council of Trent to the Code

A—*The Prescriptions of the Council of Trent*

The Council of Trent issued no direct legislation concerning the place of marriage, when, in the decree *Tametsi,* it stated the requirements for valid and licit assistance of the priest at a marriage. The parish priest could assist at the marriage of his subjects anywhere, even outside of his parish or diocese or outside of the parish church. Hence, since by the common law of the Council of Trent no determined place was prescribed for marriage, the marriage *per se* could be celebrated licitly in any decent place, whether sacred or otherwise. But since as a general rule marriages were celebrated publicly in church and with solemnity, ordinarily the parish priest could assist licitly only in his own parish church, or in another parish church with the consent of the pastor.[27] Although the words *"in facie Ecclesiae,"* as far as the form prescribed by the Council of Trent went, did not signify the material place of celebration,[28] at least the Council's wish regarding the place of celebration is shown by the wording of the decree. For the Council stated that after the banns had been published and no impediment had been discovered the celebration of marriage was to follow *in facie Ecclesiae where* the priest was to receive the mutual consent of the spouses.[29] It is evidently the mind of the Council that, as a general rule, at least, the words *in facie Ecclesiae* should be taken also to include the material edifice of the church. This is still clearer if we examine the words of the Ritual issued by Paul V in 1624. There it is stated that mar-

[27] Cf. Wernz, *Ius Matrimoniale,* n. 183.

[28] Sanchez, *De Matrimonio,* Lib. III, disp. 15, n. 20: "Ut autem dicatur Matrimonium celebrari in facie Ecclesiae, non est opus ut in ipsa Ecclesia materiali, vel in eius limine celebretur: sed satis est coram fidelium multitudine. Nam Ecclesia dicitur aliqua fidelium congregatio. Hodie autem satis dicitur contractum in facie Ecclesiae si coram parocho et duplici teste denuntiationibus praemissis matrimonium ineatur: hanc enim formam tradit Tridentinum."

[29] Sess. XXIV, *de ref. matrim.,* c. 1: ". . . quibus denunciationibus factis, si nullum legitimum opponatur impedimentum, ad celebrationem matrimonii in facie Ecclesiae procedatur, *ubi* parochus . . . etc."

riage should most fittingly be celebrated in church, but that if it should have been celebrated at the home, the spouses are to come to the church to receive the Nuptial Blessing.[30] Hence one sees that by the common law there was a counsel that marriages of the faithful be contracted in church, but that there was no prohibition, strictly so called, against their being celebrated outside the church.[31] This is borne out by the responses of the Sacred Congregations which, while they say the custom of celebrating marriages in church is a laudable one and should be retained, do not go so far as to say there is a prohibition against the celebration of marriage outside of church.[32]

It is evidently the mind of the Council then that marriage should be celebrated in the church, unless for urgent or serious reasons, the bishop should permit it to be celebrated elsewhere. This leniency, of course, applies only to the marriage contract itself and the attendant ceremonies of the Roman Ritual. If there is question of the Nuptial Blessing, which as has been seen was very rarely imparted outside of Mass, this could be received only in connection with the celebration of Mass, and hence in a church or public or semi-public oratory. There are occasional instances, however, in which permission was given the spouses to receive the Nuptial Blessing at Mass celebrated in a private oratory.[33]

B—*Legislation of Particular Councils*

Having seen that the Council of Trent made no law strictly so

[30] *Rituale Romanum*, Tit. VII, C. 1, n. 16.

[31] Gasparri, *De Matrimonio* (ed. 1904), n. 1265.

[32] S. C. Ep. et Reg. *Fulginaten.*, 6 iun. 1578: "L'Antecessore di V. S. faceva celebrare li Matrimonii nelle Chiese proprie parochiali il che era certo *multo laudabile* . . . onde questi Sigri illmi hanno voluto che se le scriva che è buona che si servi quella bona usanza. . ."—*Fontes*, n. 1334. Cf. also S. C. de Prop. Fide, Instr. (ad Vic. Ap. Scopiae), 26 sept. 1840, ad 5—*Fontes*, n. 4785; S. R. C. *Barcinon.*, 31 aug. 1872—*Fontes*, n. 6044. It is interesting to note that in regard to mission countries, where the missionary cannot be approached for the marriage ceremony, the Congregation of the Propagation of the Faith in a response of June 23, 1830, urges the spouses, when at all possible, to go to the church to exchange their consent.—*Fontes*, n. 4749.

[33] S. R. C., *Barcinon.*, 31 aug. 1872—*Fontes*, n. 6044.

called commanding that marriages be performed in church, or what amounts to the same thing, made no prohibition against marriages being held in private houses, it will now be in order to examine the legislation of particular councils held after the Council of Trent regarding the prescription that marriages be contracted in church or the prohibition that they be contracted in private houses.

Before doing so it will not be out of place to indicate a controversy between pre-Code canonists as to the power of the bishop to forbid the celebration of marriages in private houses. Barbosa held that it was beyond the bishop's power to make such a prohibition.[34] Barbosa's opinion actually deterred the Fathers of the Second Provincial Council of St. Louis, held in the year 1858, from making a strict prohibition in this regard.[35] Wernz, however, proves that such a prohibition was really within the bishop's power, since the church, while not making a strict prohibition against marriages being celebrated outside of church, did not give a special and express privilege of celebrating marriages at will outside of the church or in private houses. Had she done so, certainly such a privilege could not be curtailed. But since she had clearly shown that celebration outside of church did not please her, there was nothing to prevent the bishop by particular law from increasing the strictness of the common law. Such a particular law would be in accordance with the mind of the Church, and would serve to obtain more efficaciously the result desired by the exhortation of the common law.[36] Wernz adds that evidently bishops were not deterred from making such laws, as the legislation of many local councils attests. These councils will be considered now.

[34] *De Officio et Potestate Episcopi* (Lugduni, 1656), par. II, alleg. XXXII, n. 18.

[35] "Quarta Congregatio Privata. Adducto testimonio celeberrimi Barbosae, constitit episcopis non licere decretum emittere quo matrimonia aliter quam in ecclesiis celebrari prohibeant, latumque est decretum quo Ordinarii jubeantur fideles ad religiosam matrimonii celebrationem omnibus modis hortari."—*Coll. Lac.*, III, 316.

[36] *Ius Matrimoniale*, n. 183, notes 241 and 242. Cf. also Gasparri, *De Matrimonio* (ed. 1904), n. 1266.

Several Councils of Milan are very definite on the point that marriage is not to be performed anywhere but in the church, which is the proper place for the reception of the sacraments.[37] The Council of Benevento in 1571 has the same prescription but leaves room for the Bishop to permit otherwise.[38] The Council of Bordeaux in 1583 uses the words *in facie ecclesiae,* but it would seem from the wording of the canon that it is not used in the strictly literal sense of former days. But since the celebration of Mass and the Nuptial Blessing are mentioned, there is no doubt that the ceremony is to take place in church.[39] The Council of Rheims in the same year decrees that marriage must take place only in church unless the bishop permits otherwise.[40] The Provincial Patriarchal Council of the province of Acquitaine held at Bourges in 1584 says that the Nuptial Blessing is to be given *in facie Ecclesiae in Missa,* in the presence of two or three witnesses.[41] The Council of Toulouse states that marriage must be performed *intra Ecclesiae septa,*[42] and the Council of Aix in 1585 declares that the spouses are to be blessed after the celebration of a Mass at which they have assisted.[43] The Council of Avignon in 1594 enacts that henceforth marriage is to be celebrated not at home but in a sacred place, and that the Nuptial Blessing is to be given at Mass.[44] The Council of Narbonne in 1609 also has *"non domi, sed in loco sacro."* [45] A provincial council of Benevento in 1693 rules that the celebration is not to be permitted in private houses

[37] Conc. Mediolan, (1569)—Mansi, XXXIV A, 114; Conc. Mediolan (1573)—Mansi, XXXIV A, 168. This latter council specifies the parish church.

[38] Conc. Benevent., cap. XXIV—Mansi, XXXVI bis, 17.

[39] Tit. XV: "Benedictionem nuptialem in facie ecclesiae ante vel post Missarum celebrationem, a quarta hora matutina usque ad meridiem fieri praecipimus."—Hardouin, X, 1351.

[40] Conc. Prov. Remen. (1583), approbatum a Greg. XIII: "in ecclesia et non alibi, nisi . . . etc."—Hardouin, X, 1287.

[41] Conc. Prov. Patr. Aquitanicae celebratum Biturigibus, a. 1548—Hardouin, X, 1804.

[42] Conc. Prov. Tolosan. (1590)—Hardouin, X, 1804.

[43] Hardouin, X, 1533.

[44] C. 20—Mansi, XXXIVB, 1342.

[45] Hardouin, XI, 24.

except for a legitimate reason which must be considered and approved by the bishop, and that such a permission is not to be granted unless on the day of marriage the spouses go to confession and receive Holy Communion. As a reason for forbidding marriages at home, the council stresses the great reverence due to the sacraments.[46] An indication of the mind of the Eastern Church is shown in a ruling of the Synod of Mt. Lebanon in the year 1736, which forbids marriages in private houses or other places except the proper parish church.[47]

Around the middle of the last century there are numerous local councils which legislate that marriages should be performed in church. A council of Westminster in England in 1852 says that marriages are not to be performed in a church which does not have the care of the souls in its district.[48]

A synod of the province of Dublin in the year 1853 recalls the days of persecution in Ireland and says that in those days necessity compelled the administration of the sacraments in private houses. But now that the necessity has passed, the synod states, the practice which it generated should be abolished. The Sacraments of Baptism, Penance, and Matrimony are henceforth to be administered with all proper solemnity in the church. To this end the bishops and pastors are exhorted to ornament the church and render them fit and proper for the administration of the public rites of religion.[49]

In France the Council of Auch (1851) decreed that marriage should not be celebrated outside of the parish church,[50] and the Council of Toulouse in 1850 has a prohibtion against celebration of marriage in private oratories or outside of Mass.[51]

[46] Mansi, XXXVI ter, 591.

[47] Mansi, XXXVIII, 83.

[48] I Conc. of Westminster—*Coll. Lac.*, III, 937.

[49] Litterae Pastorales Episcoporum Provinciae Dubliniensis—*Coll. Lac.*, III, 1322. For other legislation of Irish synods on the same question see the decrees of Synod. Plenar. Episcoporum Hiberniae apud Thurles, a. 1850—*Coll. Lac.*, III, 783; Conc. Prov. Armacanae, a. 1854—*Coll. Lac.*, III, 850.

[50] *Coll. Lac.*, IV, 1191.

[51] *Coll. Lac.*, IV, 1055.

In Italy the Council of Urbino (1859) has the same prohibition.[52] The Council of Ravenna (1855) forbade marriage in even public oratories and stated that they must be performed in the parish church.[53]

The Council of Cologne (1860) in Germany stated that because of the sanctity which is inherent in it as a sacrament, marriage should be contracted only in church, unless for an extraordinary reason the bishop should dispense.[54] The Provincial Council of Utrecht (1865) in Holland says it is to be desired that marriage be performed in church, either before or after a Mass at which the spouses have received Communion.[55]

A Council of Central America in the year 1854 is very strong in its prohibtion against marriage in private houses or outside the parish church.[56] In Canada the Council of Quebec in 1854[57] and the Provincial Council of Halifax in 1857[58] command that marriage be performed in the church.

The hesitation of the Second Provincial Council of St. Louis in making a positive prohibition against marriages outside of church has already been referred to. The Fathers of the Council contented themselves with advising the bishops to urge their subjects to contract marriage in church.[59] This same hesitation is seen earlier in the Articles of Ecclesiastical Discipline, passed by the Diocesan Synod of Baltimore in 1791 and approved by the bishops of the United States in 1810.[60]

52 *Coll. Lac.*, VI, 25.

53 *Coll. Lac.*, VI, 168.

54 *Coll. Lac.*, V, 353.

55 *Coll. Lac.*, V, 841.

56 "Matrimonia benedicere in domibus privatis et extra ecclesiam paroecialem excepto infirmitatis vel gravis necessitatis causa, omnino vetitum est."—Mansi, XLVII, 65.

57 Conc. Prov. Quebec. II—*Coll. Lac.*, III, 649.

58 *Coll. Lac.*, III, 749.

59 "Hortentur Episcopi fideles sibi subditos ut matrimonia in ecclesiis, et si fieri possit, etiam intra missarum solemnia celebrentur."—*Coll Lac.*, III, 319.

60 "Cum plures occurrerent difficultates, si praescriberemus lege generali ut omnia matrimonia in Ecclesiis celebrarentur, juxta mentem et praxim

The Fathers of the First Provincial Council of New Orleans in 1856 strictly forbade the celebration of marriage outside of church, unless the parties are at a distance of at least three miles from any church.[61] The Pastoral Letter of the Second Plenary Council of Baltimore stresses the importance of contracting marriage before the altar of God, but does not express a clear prohibition against the contrary practice.[62]

From the numerous prohibitions enumerated above it is evident that most bishops were not deterred by the opinion of Barbosa from forbidding marriages to be performed outside of church, as the Fathers of the St. Louis Council were. And in making such a prohibition they were in accord with the mind of the Church, as has been stated above.

orbis Catholici, praematuram judicavimus hac de re aliquid decernere. Verum omnes Pastores admonemus ut hanc piam consuetudinem fidelibus commendent, eorumque animos ad eam brevi tempore amplectendam disponant."—*Coll. Lac.*, III, 8.

[61] "Cum sacramenta propter reverentiam eis debitam, in loco sancto debeant ministrari, Patres Concilii . . . omnio prohibent ne sacramenta baptismi et matrimonii extra ecclesiam celebrentur, nisi locus tribus saltem miliariis ab omni ecclesia distet."—*Coll. Lac.*, III, 242.

[62] ". . . Non possums vobis nimium inculcare, qnanti referat, illud ante altare Dei nec sine sacri nuptialis caerimonia contrahi; ut qui sanctum hoc jugum subeunt, peculiarem illam benedictionem et inde profluentem divinae opis abundantiam percipiant, qua instructi gravissimis officiis satisfacere possint."—*Coll. Lac.*, III, 1262.

CHAPTER IV

THE CELEBRATION OF MIXED MARRIAGES

The purpose of this chapter is to prepare the historical background for Chapter VIII which will comment on the law of canons 1102, § 2, and 1109, § 3, which enjoin that mixed marriages shall be celebrated outside of church and without any sacred rites. Hence this chapter will concern itself primarily with the development of legislation regarding the exclusion of a religious celebration of mixed marriages.

From the fourth century on the marriages of the faithful with aliens to the Faith were universally forbidden.[1] Since, from the time of the Decretals to the so-called Reformation there were many laws, canonical and civil, inflicting severe penalties on heretics, there were very few laws directed especially against mixed marriages.[2] As Schenk observes, because of the severe discipline of the late Middle Ages against heretics and heresy, and the stringent laws against all association with the unbaptized (Jews and Saracens), the possibility of entering such marriages was not even discussed.[3]

But with the advent of the political and religious changes brought about by the pseudo-Reformation, and because of the missionary activity aroused by the discovery of the New World, the question of marriages with those not of the Faith became a live one. In regard to the missions the Church took the new conditions into account and permitted the apostolic vicars of mission lands to dispense, with proper safeguards, from the impediment of disparity of cult, in order that the spread of the Faith might be fostered.[4]

[1] Schenk, *The Matrimonial Impediments of Mixed Religion and Disparity of Cult,* The Catholic University of America Canon Law Studies, n. 51 (Washington, D. C., 1929), p. 29. Hereafter this work will be cited as *Mixed Religion & Disparity of Cult.*

[2] Wernz, *Ius Matrimoniale,* n. 576.

[3] *Mixed Religion & Disparity of Cult,* p. 44.

[4] Schenk, *op. cit.,* pp. 46-47.

In Europe, however, heresy was making sweeping inroads in many countries. The ancient prescriptions against mixed marriages had again to be renewed and enforced since Catholics were becoming imbued with the principles of reformers, and especially with a spirit of religious indifferentism.[5] It is easy to see why the Church could not permit a heretic to marry a Catholic. This would seem equivalent to the acknowledgment of the right of the new heresy of Protestantism to exist. Pope Clement VIII interdicted mixed marriages altogether in Italy.[6] The Church would not dispense from the impediment of mixed religion unless the abjuration of heresy preceded. Where the abjuration of heresy did not take place the Church would not dispense execept for reasons of a manifest public concern, i.e. for the marriages of Catholic rulers with some one of their rank but of a heretical form of religion.[7]

In spite of this severe discipline many variations in practice existed in those countries which had become infected with Protestantism. Mixed marriages were being entered into by the common people without a dispensation and without any abjuration of heresy. This practice led some eminent canonists to hold that in these countries the impediment of mixed religion had become obsolete by custom.[8] To quote Oesterle: "The distinctive characteristic of this period (from the Council of Trent to 1782) is one of confusion concerning the theological principles regarding mixed marriages, and consequently one of confusion regarding the practical question of the manner of assistance at such marriage by the Catholic priest." [9]

Gradually, however, the Church's discipline in the matter of mixed marriage began to take definite form. She no longer re-

[5] Feije, *Dissertatio Canonica de Matrimoniis Mixtis* (Lovanii, 1847), p. 3. Hereafter this work will be cited as *De Matr. Mixtis.*

[6] Const. *Cum sicut,* 26 iulii 1596—*Bullarum Diplomatum et Privilegiorum Romanorum Pontificum Taurinensis Editio* (24 vols. and appendix, Augustae Taurinorum, 1857-1872), X, 279.

[7] Shenk, *Mixed Religion and Disparity of Cult,* p. 47.

[8] Schenk, *op. cit.,* pp. 49-50, and note 13.

[9] Oesterle, "Circa Declarationem Authenticam Can. 1102 De Passiva Assistentia,"—*Jus Pontificium,* X (1930), 110-119, 292-314, esp. p. 304.

quired a *causa publica* or the abjuration of heresy as conditions for dispensing. Serious reasons of a private nature sufficed, but guarantees must be given which safeguarded the Faith of the Catholic party and of the future offspring. Rather than dispense from these *cautiones* the Church continued to tolerate the practice that existed in certain places of permitting the passive assistance of the pastor, without asking and receiving the consent of the parties.[10] The Popes from Benedict XIV to Pius IX reiterated the Church's attitude towards mixed marriages and insisted that they should not be permitted unless a dispensation had been obtained and the necessary *cautiones* had been given.[11] In all the letters of the popes and in the responses of the Sacred Congregations it is repeated again and again that the Church has always detested mixed marriages because of the danger which they create to the Faith of the Catholic party and of the future offspring, and because of the *communicatio in sacris* which they entail.

Lest she should seem in dispensing to approve of such unions the Holy See, in all the above mentioned letters and responses, forbade all liturgical rites in the celebration of mixed marriages, and insisted that they should be contracted outside of church. It was only to avoid greater evils that she would permit some sort of religious celebration at mixed marriages. A survey, in chronological order, of the letters of the popes and of the replies of the Sacred Congregations on this matter will be useful as a background to Chapter VIII of this work.

In Belgium the civil law had enacted the enforced assistance of pastors at mixed marriages. Pope Pius VI (1775-1799) in a rescript to the Cardinal Archbishop of Malines said that if the

[10] Schenk, *Mixed Religion and Disparity of Cult,* pp. 63-64. On page 64, note 59, he notes that the term "passive assistance" as used above is used in the strict sense, namely, *audito consensu.* The instructions of the Holy See sometimes used the term in a broader sense, i.e., in the sense of forbidding any active cooperation by the use of liturgical rites or the publication of the banns.

[11] So rigid were the popes in dispensing from the impediment of mixed religion that it was not till the end of the eigtheenth century or the beginning of the nineteenth that they subdelegated this faculty to the bishops. Cf. Schenk, *op. cit.,* p. 61.

Catholic party could not be deterred from contracting a mixed marriage, the priest could assist passively provided that the guarantees required by divine law were given, and provided moreover that the marriage be not performed in church, or with religious ceremonies.[12] An Instruction of the Propaganda to the vicar apostolic of Sweden in 1785 says the priest, due to circumstances in Sweden, should not ordinarily assist at mixed marriages. But if the danger of the perversion of the Catholic party is removed, and the promises are made to bring up all the children in the Catholic religion, then the priest's assistance can be tolerated. He is to lend only his material presence, and the marriage is to be performed outside of church and without the prayers prescribed by the Ritual.[13] A reply of the Holy Office to the Archbishop of Quebec reprobates a practice which is alleged to have come into vogue in the United States, namely, that of imparting the Nuptial Blessing—it is not clear that the solemn Nuptial Blessing is meant—at mixed marriages. Such marriages are permitted after the necessary guarantees have been given, but they can never be performed in church, nor can they be celebrated with the blessing of the priest or with any sacred rite.[14] The same congregation when asked if it was lawful to pronounce the form prescribed by the Ritual, and to say the prayers there prescribed, and to bless the ring, responded in the negative.[15]

An instruction of the Holy Office in 1824 to the Archbishop of Quebec takes up the question of an infidel woman married to a heretic. The woman wishes to become a Catholic. Since the existing marriage is invalid because of disparity of worship, the Archbishop is in a dilemma: should he permit the woman after

[12] Pius VI, rescript. ad Card. Archiep. Mechlinien., 13 iul. 1782, n. 4—*Fontes*, n. 471. Oesterle (*Jus Pont.*, X [1930], 110, note 3) says this is the first clear example of passive assistance found in the sources. For a more complete exposition of the situation in Belgium at the time of the Pope's letter cf. the same author (*art. cit.*). See also Schenk, *Mixed Religion and Disparity of Cult*, pp. 58-60.

[13] S. C. de Prop. Fide, instr. (ad Vic. Ap. Sveciae), 6 sept. 1785—*Fontes*, n. 4606.

[14] S. C. S. Off. (Quebec), 10 sept. 1820—*Fontes*, n. 859.

[15] S. C. S. Off., 1 aug. 1821—*Fontes*, n. 863.

baptism to remarry the man before a minister; should he refuse to baptize the woman, thus possibly causing her to be baptized by a non-Catholic minister; or finally should he baptize her and join her in wedlock to the man even though this implied a *communicatio in sacris?* The Holy Office replied that the woman was to be baptized and the priest was to officiate at the marriage with two witnesses, but the ceremony was to take place outside of church, without the Nuptial Blessing and without any sacred rite whatsoever.[16]

Pius VIII (31 March, 1829-1 Dec., 1830), in a letter to the Archbishop of Cologne and the Bishops of Treves, Münster and Paderborn regarding the special difficulty which had arisen in Germany due to the enactment of a law which required all the children of a marriage to be educated in the religion of the father or according to his wish, declared that, to avoid greater evils to the Catholic position in Germany, the pastor could permit the parties of the mixed marriage to exchange their consent before him, and could register the marriage in the parish register, but he must never by any act whatsoever appear to approve such a marriage, and what is more, he must abstain from reciting any prayers or performing any ecclesiastical rite in connection with the marriage.[17] An Instruction of the Secretaries of State was issued two days later regarding the same dioceses. It granted a *sanatio in radice* for all marriages entered into without the form of the Council of Trent up to the date of the Instruction. From then on the form of the Council does not bind in these four dioceses.. The bishop, in the case of a mixed marriage in these dioceses, when the *cautiones* are not given, can dispense in writing from diriment impediments. But since these marriages are gravely sinful, the priest must not only refrain from honoring such marriages by any ecclesiastical rite whatsoever, but he must also abstain from any act by which he might seem to approve such unions.[18]

[16] S. C. S. Off., instr. (ad Archiep. Quebecen.), 16 sept. 1824, ad 5 —*Fontes*, n. 866.

[17] Pius VIII, litt. ap., *Litteras altero*, 25 mart. 1830—*Fontes*, n. 482.

[18] Instr. Secret. Status (Card. Albani), 27 mart., 1830—*Fontes*, n. 6451.

Gregory XVI (1831-1846), in a letter to the Bishops of Hungary, stated that if a mixed marriage in which the guarantees were not given could not be averted without danger of greater evil and scandal, and if at the same time it would be to the advantage of the Church and the good of souls that such a marriage, though gravely sinful, should be entered into before the priest rather than before an heretical minister, the priest could assist, but only passively, by his material presence alone, and he must abstain from any ecclesiastical rite whatsoever.[19] The same Pope, in a letter to the Bishop of Freiburg declared that it was the custom of the Church not to impart a blessing even at those mixed marriages which had been entered into with papal dispensation and after the customary guarantees had been given. And although the custom of blessing such marriages which had arisen in some places could be tolerated, such a blessing must never be imparted in the case of a mixed marriage entered into without the Church's permission, and without the customary guarantees. Such an act would be a tacit approval of a marriage which is gravely sinful at its very outset.[20]

An important document on the celebration of mixed marriages is the so called *Instructio Antonelliana* issued in the year 1858 by Pius IX (1846-1878) through his Secretary of State, Cardinal Antonelli. Since this Instruction forms the basis of the law of the Code as expressed in canons 1102, § 2, and 1109, § 3, it will be discussed in full in Chapter VIII of the Canonical Commentary,[21] along with a letter of the Holy Office [22] and one from the Congregation for the Propagation of the Faith,[23] both of which explained more fully the *Instructio Antonelliana*.

In 1872 the Holy Office was asked whether the phrase *exclusa*

[19] Greg. XVI, Litt. ap., ad episcopos Hungariae, *Quas vestro*, 30 apr. 1841—*Fontes*, n. 497.

[20] Greg. XVI, epist. *Non sine gravi*, 23 maii 1846—*Fontes*, n. 503.

[21] Secret. Status, instr. 15 nov. 1858, iussu Pii Papae IX—*Fontes*, n. 6454. Cf. *infra*, pp. 117-118.

[22] S. C. S. Off. litt. (ad Vic. Ap. Myssurien.) 26 nov. 1862—*Fontes*, n. 971. Cf. *infra, pp.* 130-131, note 59.

[23] S. C. de Prop. Fide, littl. encyl., 11 mart. 1868—*Fontes*, n. 4872. Cf *infra*, p. 119, note 21.

semper Missae celebratione found in rescripts applying to mixed marriages forbade only the Nuptial Mass, or also any private Mass which was celebrated in the presence of the spouses and the bridal party after the marriage had been contracted, even though no special place in church was assigned to the bride and groom. The Supreme Congregation replied in the affirmative to both questions, when the celebration of the Mass, could be considered from the circumstances as a complement to the marriage ceremony.[24]

The Bishop of St. Albert laid before the Holy Office the case of certain poorly instructed Catholics in his diocese who were reached by the missionary only once or twice a year. Their condition was one of extreme poverty. Their surroundings were entirely Protestant. They were prone to contract mixed marriages due to their lack of instruction they could not understand why the missionary looked with disfavor on their entering such unions. When, in assisting at such marriages, he refrained from using any religious ceremony, they interpreted this omission as an indication that he despised them because of their poverty. The Protestant ministers used this attitude of mind as a means of drawing these ignorant Catholics away from the Faith. The bishop asked the faculty of employing some religious ceremony in these mixed marriages or at least permission to use the surplice when assisting at such weddings. The Holy Office referred to the *Instructio Antonelliana* which empowered the bishop to permit the use of sacred rites at mixed marriages, when greater evils would follow if they were refused. But since there was a danger that these poorly instructed Catholics might become convinced that the Church was not opposed to mixed marriages if too much leniency were shown in the matter of sacred rites, the bishop was urged to be very cautious in the use of the power granted him by the *Instructio*. The use of the surplice alone was to be permitted, unless the employment of some religious ceremony was deemed

[24] S. C. S. Off., 17 ian. 1872, ad I—*Fontes*, n. 1020.

necessary, in the prudent judgment of the bishop, to prevent the defection of these Catholics from the Faith.[25]

The Holy Office was asked in 1885 whether a mixed marriage could be held in church after the Blessed Sacrament had been removed; whether the priest could wear a surplice and stole; and whether, before or after the marriage, the priest could give a short sermon on the sanctity and indissolubility of marriage. The Holy Office referred to the Instruction of 1858, and, regarding the sermon, left that to the judgement of the bishop.[26]

In all this legislation on the celebration of mixed marriages, there is seen underlying the whole mass of legislation the Church's purpose, namely to keep alive in the mind of the faithful the knowledge of the ancient law which condemns mixed marriages, and her zealous desire to save her children from such dangerous unions, so fraught with peril to the Faith and the eternal salvation of both the Catholic party and the children possibly to be born of such marriages.

[25] S. C. S. Off. instr. (ad ep. S. Alberti), 9 dec. 1874, n. 18—*Fontes*, n. 1034.

[26] S. C. S. Off. *(Rosen.)*, 16 iulii 1885—*Fontes*, n. 1094.

PART II

CANONICAL COMMENTARY

Chapter V

THE LITURGICAL FORM OF MARRIAGE

Chapter VI of the Code's Title on Matrimony bears the rubric *De forma celebrationis matrimonii.* From the contents of this chapter of the Code it is evident that the word "form" is used in the rubric in a broad sense, and that it includes *all* the solemnities prescribed by ecclesiastical law for the celebration of marriage. Some of these solemnities, however, have direct reference to marriage in so far as it is a contract, while others regard rather its sacramental character. The solemnities, the observance of which the Church's law prescribes in order that marriage in its contractual aspect may be validly and lawfully celebrated, may be called the "juridical form of marriage," or simply the "form of marriage," in the sense in which it is used in canon 1099.

Some of the solemnities of the juridical form of marriage are demanded for the valid celebration of marriage some are required for its lawful celebration. Hence the juridical form may be divided into the substantial form, namely, that which is required for validity, and the accidental form, namely, that which is prescribed for lawfulness.

The substantial form is set forth in canons 1094 to 1096 inclusively. Canon 1094 gives the general principle that only those marriages are valid which are contracted before the pastor, or the local ordinary (or their delegate), and two witnesses. Canons 1095 and 1096 give the conditions required for valid assistance on the part of the pastor or the local ordinary, or the priest delegated by them.

The accidental juridical form, namely, the requirments for lawful assistance, is set forth in canon 1097. Canon 1098 gives two cases in which the presence of two witnesses alone is sufficient to satisfy the law on the form, provided that the presence of the pastor, of the local ordinary, or of the properly delegated priest, is impossible or cannot be had without serious inconvenience, namely, in danger of death, or when it is foreseen that the proper priest cannot be had for a month. Canon 1099 lists those who are bound by the Catholic form of marriage, and those who are exempt from this form.

Besides the solemnities prescribed for the juridical form, there are others which have direct reference to marriage in so far as it is a sacrament. These may be called the "liturgical form of marriage." In so far as it is understood independently of the asking and receiving of the consent of the parties by the pastor or the local ordinary, this liturgical form has nothing to do with the validity of marriage. The omission or mutilation of it in no way affects the validity of the marriage.

The ceremonies of this liturgical form are of two classes. 1. The sacred rites surrounding the exchange of consent, which are commanded by the Church and which are to be performed according to the Roman Ritual or the diocesan ritual. These rites have no necessary connection with the Holy Sacrifice. They are called (along with the exchange of consent) *ritus copulationis,* or *ritus celebrationis,* or *benedictio nuptialis simplex.* 2. Certain sacred rites of a more solemn character, which are not obligatory, or at most *sub levi,* performed according to the Roman Missal, and during the Sacrifice of the Mass. These rites are called *benedictio nuptialis sollemnis,* or merely *benedictio nuptialis.* The rite of celebration or of the simple blessing is treated in canon 1100 of the Code; the rite of the solemn blessing is treated in canon 1101. This chapter, then, will comprise two articles, the one devoted to the form of the Ritual blessing, and the other to that of the solemn blessing as contained in the Missal.

Article I

THE RITE OF CELEBRATION

Canon 1100. Extra casum necessitatis, in matrimonii celebratione serventur ritus in libris ritualibus ab Ecclesia praescripti aut laudabilibus consuetudinibus recepti.

The rite of celebration consists in those ceremonies and prayers which, in conjunction with the exchange of consent, are found in the Roman Ritual or in a diocesan ritual. Sometimes these ceremonies are called the simple Nuptial Blessing in contradistinction to the solemn Nuptial Blessing, which is the Nuptial Blessing properly so called, contained in the Roman Missal. The ceremonies of the Roman Ritual may be divided into four groups: 1) the questions by which the mutual consent is asked and received, according to the norm established by canon 1095, § 1, 3°; 2) the joining of the hands while the words *"Ego conjungo vos, etc."* are pronounced by the priest; 3) the blessing of the ring; 4) certain prayers, namely, some versicles and responses, the ***Pater noster***, other versicles and responses, and the oration ***"Respice** quaesumus."*

That this rite of celebration is of obligation is clear from the wording of canon 1100: "Outside of the case of necessity, the rites prescribed in the rituals approved by the Church, or those rites which have been introduced by laudable custom, shall be observed in the celebration of marriage." The words ***serventur ritus*** express a genuine law, and not merely a counsel. Therefore when the mutual matrimonial consent is exchanged, the sacred rites prescribed by the Roman Ritual or approved by laudable custom must be observed. The only exception is the case of necessity, for example, when times does not permit, as when one of the parties is in danger of death. The lack of a competent priest to assist at the marriage, in the circumstances stated by canon 1098, would be another example of a case of necessity.

While the Code commands that sacred rites be used in conjunction with the juridical form of marriage, still in accordance with the principle expressed in canon 2,[1] it does not in its text outline the specific rites to be employed, but indicates the rites prescribed by the Ritual or such rites as have been introduced by laudable custom. Therefore, besides the rites prescribed by the Roman Ritual, which are substantially to be retained, the rites introduced

[1] "Codex, plerumque, nihil decernit de ritibus et caeremoniis quas liturgici libri, ab Ecclesia Latina probati, servandas praecipiunt in celebratione sacrosancti Missae sacrficii, in administratione Sacramentorum et Sacramentalium aliisque sacris peragendis. Quare omnes liturgicae leges vim suam retinent, nisi earum aliqua in Codice expresse corrigatur."

by laudable custom are to be kept also.[2] Therefore a pastor would not be justified in changing the rites approved by custom.

As a general rule the rites prescribed for the celebration of marriage are of obligation, and this obligation binds both the assisting priest and the spouses. There are cases, however, when these sacred rites of the Ritual are not obligatory, but rather optional; and finally there are cases in which all sacred rites are disallowed.

There are two instances in which the ceremonies of the Ritual must be employed. The first is that of two Catholics, who here and now contract marriage in accordance with the juridical form outlined by canon 1094. In this case the liturgical form as found in the Ritual must also be employed. The sacred ceremonies of the Ritual must be used in their entirety. It makes no difference whether it is the first or a later time that either of the parties contracts marriage, whether the woman is a widow or the man is a widower.[3]

[2] Such customs vary with different localities. It appears neither necessary nor particularly useful to attempt even a partial enumeration. The following authors give examples of such customs: Payen, *De Matrimonio in Missionibus ac Potissimum in Sinis Tractatus Practicus et Casus* (3 vols., 2. ed., Zi-ka-wei: in Typographia T'ou-se-we, 1936), II, 253, note 1 to be cited hereafter as *De Matrimonio*); Wernz-Vidal, *Ius Canonicum* 7 vols. in 8 Vol. V [*Ius Matrimoniale*], Romae: Apud Aedes Universitatis Gregorianae, 1925), V, p. 651, note 6,—p. 653, note 12—p. 654, note 15 (Hereafter cited as *Ius Matrimoniale*); De Smet, *Tractatus Theologico-Canonicus de Sponsalibus et Matrimonio* (4. ed., Brugis: Car. Beyaert, 1927), p. 168, note 1 (Hereafter cited as *De Spons. et Mat.*); Vlaming, *Praelectiones Iuris Matrimonii* (3. ed., 2 vols., Bussum in Hollandia: Sumptibus Societatis Editricis Anonymae olim Paulus Brand, 1919-1921), n. 610 (Hereafter cited as *Praelectiones*); Cappello, *Tractatus Canonico-Moralis de Sacramentis* (3 vols. in 6, Vol. III [*De Matrimonio*], 4. ed., Romae: Apud Aedes Univ. Gregorianae, 1939), n. 705 (Hereafter cited as *De Matrimonio*); O'Kane-Fallon, *Notes on the Rubrics of the Roman Ritual* (new ed., Dublin: James Duffey & Co., Ltd., 1938), pp. 552-563. The latter work gives some of the customs in vogue in England, Ireland and the United States.

[3] S. C. S. Off., instr. (ad Praef. Mission. Martinicae etc.), 6 iul. 1817—*Fontes*, n. 855; S. C. de Prop. Fide (C. P. pro Sin.-Sutchuen.), 20 feb. 1801—*Fontes*, n. 4666; S. C. de Prop. Fide, instr. (ad Vic. Gen. Nankin.),

In the case of a convalidation in which the renewal of consent is made in the proper juridical form Brennan states that it should be accompanied by the marriage ceremony as it is found in the Ritual. He notes that if the ring had been blessed at a former ceremony it is not to be blessed again. If the consent is renewed in a quasi-private manner, i.e., in the presence of the pastor and the witnesses only, the ceremonies of the Ritual may or may not be employed at the option of the parties and the pastor.[4]

The second case in which the rites of the Ritual are to be used is that of two Catholics who have contracted marriage validly without the juridical form of canon 1094, either because they were exempted from it by the law of canon 1098, or because they were dispensed by the ordinary, the pastor, etc. in accordance with the provisions of canons 1043 and 1044.[5] Catholics who have contracted marriage in this way must, if and when the opportunity presents itself, come before the pastor that the liturgical form of the Ritual may be supplied. The pastor is to instruct the couple, however, that these rites are not necessary for the validity of their marriage; he is also to refrain from asking and receiving

29 feb. 1836—*Fontes,* n. 4761; S. C. de Prop. Fide, 21 sept. 1843—*Fontes,* n. 4802; S. R. C., Rhedonen., 27 aug. 1836, ad 2—*Fontes,* n. 5881.

[4] Brennan, *The Simple Convalidation of Marriage,* The Catholic University of America Canon Law Studies, n. 102 (Washington, D. C.: The Catholic University of America, 1937), Article 3, *The Liturgical Form in Convalidation,* pp. 94-96.

[5] Can. 1098: "Si haberi vel adiri nequeat sine gravi incommodo parochus vel loci Ordinarius vel sacerdos delegatus qui matrimonio assistant ad normam canonum 1095, 1096:

1° In mortis periculo validum et licitum est matrimonium contractum coram solis testibus; et etiam extra mortis periculum, dummodo prudenter praevideatur eam rerum conditionem esse per mensem duraturam;

2° In utroque casu, si praesto sit alius sacerdos qui adesse possit, vocari et, una cum testibus, matrimonio assistere debet, salva coniugiii validitate coram solis testibus."

Can. 1043: "Urgente mortis periculo, locorum Ordinarii . . . possunt super forma in matrimonii celebratione servanda . . . dispensare . . ."

Can. 1044: ". . . eadem dispensandi facultate pollet tum parochus, tum sacerdos qui matrimonio, ad normam can. 1098, n. 2, assistit, tum confessarius. . ."

the consent of the parties, and from pronouncing the words, *"Ego conjungo vos, etc."* The case contemplated is more likely to occur in missionary countries, namely, in those localities which the missionary reaches only at rare intervals, as is seen from the sources which contain legislation regarding this matter.[6]

Authors agree that there is an obligation of supplying the Ritual ceremonies in the case just mentioned. Gasparri says the obligation is a serious one. He admits that no serious obligation can be deduced from the Code, but says that several responses of the Sacred Congregations seem to indicate such a serious obligation.[7] He is opposed by Cappello, who more correctly says that under the present law there is no clear indication of a serious precept. Taking into consideration canon 22 and canon 1098, which latter canon completely readjusts the subject matter of the former law, Cappello says that the responses of the Sacred Congregations do not offer a peremptory argument for the presence of a serious obligation.[8]

Regarding the case of two infidels married validly in infidelity, and afterwards converted to the Catholic Church, the Holy Office, in a reply of June 26, 1860, stated that while it was very praiseworthy and advantageous for them to receive the blessings (i.e., of the Ritual and of the Missal) of the Church on their marriage, however, they were not to be compelled to receive them.[9] The

[6] S.C.S. Off. (Sutchuen.) 15 ian. 1874—*Fontes,* n. 846; S.C.S. Off., instr. (ad Praef. Mission. Martinicae etc.), 6 iul. 1817—*Fontes,* n. 855; S.C.S. Off. (Coreae), 26 iun. 1860, ad 2—*Fontes,* n. 961; S.C.de Prop. Fide, instr. a. 1806—*Fontes,* n. 4683; S.C. de Prop. Fide, instr. (ad Vic. Ap. Sin.), 23 iun. 1830—*Fontes,* n. 4749; S.C. de Prop. Fide, instr. (ad Vic. Gen. Nankin), 29 feb. 1836—*Fontes,* n. 4761. The case mentioned in some of these sources, namely, the supplying of the ceremonies in marriages which had been contracted clandestinely, is no longer possible since the *Ne temere,* Cf. S.C.C., decr. *"Ne temere,"* 2 aug. 1907—*Fontes,* n. 4340.

[7] *Tractatus Canonicus de Matrimonio* (ed. nova ad mentem Codicis I. C., 2 vols., Romae: Typis Polyglottis Vaticanis, 1932), nn. 1033-1037. This post-Code work of Gasparri will be cited hereafter as *De Matrimonio* (ed. nova).

[8] *De Matrimonio,* n. 708.

[9] S.C.S. Off. (Coreae), ad 1—*Fontes,* n. 961.

same principle would also apply to a mixed marriage, contracted after obtaining a dispensation from the impediment of mixed religion or of disparity of worship, upon the non-Catholic party's-subsequent conversion. In these cases the parties are to be told that the ceremony is not required for the validity of their marriage, the priest is to refrain from asking and receiving their consent, and from pronouncing the words, *"Ego coniungo vos, etc."*

In the reply of the Holy Office just mentioned there was an answer to a second question. It was asked if anything should be done by way of supplying the ceremonies of marriage upon the request of the parties of the marriage, if one of the parties still continued in paganism. The answer was given in the negative.[10] Another instance wherein the employment of the Ritual ceremonies is disallowed is had in the case of mixed marriages, as the Code expressly states in Canon 1102, § 2. This provision will be treated at length in the final chapter of this work.

As has been noted, except for the case of necessity, there is an obligation on the part of the pastor to observe in the celebration of marriage the sacred ceremonies of the Ritual or those rites which stand approved by laudable custom, and there is an obligation on the part of the spouses to demand these ceremonies when their marriage is celebrated. The rites commanded by the Church in the administration of the sacraments cannot be ignored without sin, and these ceremonies of the Ritual are the rites which the Church prescribes in the reception of the sacrament of matrimony. It would be a serious sin for the priest to omit the interrogation of the parties regarding their consent, for this interrogation is required for the validity of the matrimonial contract. It would be a grave sin likewise to omit all the other ceremonies of the Ritual. The wilful omission of one or the other of these ceremonies would constitute at least a venial sin. Of course a case of necessity would excuse from all the accidental ceremonies of the Ritual, for example, the case provided for by canon 1098, or the case in which one of the parties is in danger of death and there is no time to supply the ceremonies of the Ritual.[11]

[10] S.C.S. Off. (Coreae), 26 iun. 1860, ad 2—*Fontes,* n. 961.
[11] Gasparri, *De Matrimonio* (ed. 1932), n. 1032.

It would be beyond the scope of a canonical treatise to describe at length the Ritual ceremonies for the celebration of marriage. These ceremonies are found in the revised edition of the Roman Ritual, under chapter two of title seven.[12] The works of the standard canonical writers on matrimony give much useful information concerning these Ritual ceremonies of marriage.[13]

ARTICLE II

THE RITE OF THE SOLEMN BLESSING

Canon 1101

§ 1. Parochus curet ut sponsi benedictionem sollemnem accipiant, quae dari eis potest etiam postquam diu vixerint in matrimonio, sed solum in Missa, servata speciali rubrica et excepto tempore feriato.

§ 2. Sollemnem benedictionem ille tantum sacerdos per se ipse vel per alium dare potest, qui valide et licite matrimonio potest assistere.

The above canon contains the Code's law regarding the Nuptial Blessing properly so called in contradistinction to the simple blessing of the Ritual. Paragraph one outlines the pastor's duty in this matter, and reflects the Church's mind that all Catholics, whenever it is possible, should receive this solemn blessing of the Church on their marriage. "The pastor shall see to it that the spouses receive the Solemn Blessing. This may be given them even after they have lived a long time in the married state, but it may be imparted only during Mass, and with the observance of the special rubric. It cannot be given during the closed time."

[12] *Rituale Romanum (ad normam Codicis)*, Tit. VII, *De Sacramento Matrimonii*, Caput 2, *Ritus Celebrandi Matrimonii Sacramentum.* For the rites *laudabilibus consuetudinibus recepti* in the United States, cf. *The Priest's New Ritual* (compiled by Rev. Paul Griffith, Baltimore: John Murphy, 1940).

[13] Cf. Gasparri, *Di Matrimonio* (ed. nova), nn. 1039-1042; Cappello, *De Matrimonio,* n. 705; Payen, *De Matrimonio,* nn. 1858-1862; Wernz-Vidal, *Ius Matrimoniale, n.* 555; Rossi, *De Matrimonii Celebratione* (Romae: Pustet, 1924), n. 95.

Paragraph two states the pastor's rights regarding the Nuptial Blessing: "The solemn Nuptial Blessing may be given only by the priest who has the right to witness the marriage validly and licitly, or by his delegate."

To facilitate the understanding of canon 1108, which will be treated in the following chapter, it will be useful to summarize in the present article the legal prescriptions regarding the solemn blessing. This article will consider the following points: A) a description of the rite of solemn blessing; B) the obligation of imparting and requesting the solemn blessing; C) the minister of the solemn blessing; D) the subject of the solemn blessing; E) the votive Mass *pro sponso et sponsa;* F) the Mass of the day (said on the days which exclude the votive Nuptial Mass).

A—*Ceremonies of the Solemn Blessing*

The Church has always regarded the Sacrifice of the Mass as the most fitting setting for her most important events, such as the ordination of priests, the consecration of churches, etc. To show her high regard for the sacrament of matrimony she has inserted among the votive Masses of the Missal the *Missa pro sponso et sponsa,* composed of passages from Holy Scripture suitable for and appropriate to the Sacrament of Matrimony, and containing the three prayers which comprise the Nuptial Blessing, the Church's public official blessing on the marriage already contracted.[14] The Sacrifice of the Mass is interrupted after the *Pater Noster* and the first two of these prayers, namely, the *Propitiare, Domine,* and the *Deus, qui potestate,* are said over the newly married couple. The third prayer, *Deus Abraham,* is said after the *Benedicamus Domino* or the *Ite missa est.* These three prayers, then, comprise essentially the solemn Nuptial Blessing. They are said at the places indicated, even if the rubrics do not permit the votive Nuptial Mass to be said. While it is highly desirable that the married couple should receive Communion during the rite of the solemn

[14] S.R.C., *Romana,* 9 maii, 1893, ad III: "Benedictio nuptialis consistit in orationibus quae habentur in missali: Propitiare, Domine etc. et Deus, qui potestate etc. dicendae ante Libera nos etc.; nec non Deus Abraham etc. dicenda ante benedictionem."—*Fontes,* n. 6226.

blessing, and while the priest should strongly urge them to do so, however there is no strict precept in this matter, and the solemn blessing can be imparted even if the married couple does not receive Communion during the Mass.[15]

B—*The Obligation of Imparting and Requesting the Solemn Blessing*

Is there a strict precept regarding the Nuptial Blessing, or merely a counsel that it be received? To answer this question a distinction must be made. With regard to the spouses there is most probably no strict obligation to receive the Nuptial Blessing. The pastor, certainly, has some obligation, at least *sub levi,* to administer the solemn blessing.

1—The Spouses

All authors agree that the spouses would sin if they neglected the Nuptial Blessing through contempt or indifference. This follows from the general principles of moral theology. But it is a disputed question whether there is a strict obligation for the parties to ask for and to receive the solemn blessing. Some authors, basing their argument on an instruction of the Holy Office,[16] say that the spouses are bound *sub levi* to ask for the solemn blessing at their marriage or at least shortly thereafter, provided that they are capable of receiving it.[17] They admit that the obligation ceases if there is an excusing cause, or if the parties have been married for a notable length of time.

But other authors think that as far as the spouses are concerned the Nuptial Blessing is a matter rather of counsel than of strict obligation.[18] This seems the better opinion since the replies of

[15] S.R.C., *Lavantina,* 21 mart. 1874—*Fontes,* n. 6063.

[16] S.C.S. Off., instr. (ad Praef. Mission. Martinicae etc.), 6 iul. 1817—*Fontes,* n. 855.

[17] Vlaming, *Praelectiones,* n. 744, p. 218; Aertnys-Damen, *Theologia Moralis* (12. ed., 4. post codicem, 2 vols., Taurinorum Augustae: Marietti, 1932), II, n. 850.

[18] Gasparri, *De Matrimonio* (ed. nova), n. 1049; Chelodi, *Ius Matrimoniale* (4. ed., Tridenti: Libreria Moderna Editrice A. Ardesi, 1937), n. 145.

the Sacred Congregations seem to impose a precept only with regard to the simple blessing of the Ritual. They speak of a blessing which will counteract the scandal arising from clandestine marriages.[19] Furthermore the Sacred Congregation of Rites stated in its general decree on votive Masses that the spouses were not to be forced, but rather urged, to receive the Nuptial Blessing.[20]

Hence all authors agree that there is no serious obligation on the part of the spouses to seek the Nuptial Blessing.[21] Indeed, in the light of the instructions of the Sacred Congregations and of the dispute among the authors, it is most probable that there is not even a slight obligation on the part of the spouses.

2—The Pastor

The pastor has a twofold duty in the matter of the Nuptial Blessing. He is bound, generally *sub levi,* to impart the Nuptial Blessing to all who ask for it. He also has an obligation (again *sub levi*) of seeing to it (*curare debet*) that Catholics receive this blessing at their marriages or shortly thereafter.

Regarding the first duty, the pastor "who can validly and licitly witness the marriage" is bound to impart the Nuptial Blessing on the day the marriage is celebrated, or later on,[22] to all the couples who ask for it, provided that they are not forbidden to receive it by the prescriptions of canons 1102, § 2, 1108, § 2, or 1143. The blessing can be given even if it is known that the parties who ask for it are not in the state of grace. It is not to be denied to a woman who has been married for a considerable length of time even though she has already borne children, or is pregnant at the

[19] S.C.S. Off., instr. (ad Praef. Mission. Martinicae etc.), 6 iul. 1817—*Fontes,* n. 855; S.C. de Prop. Fide, instr. (ad Vic. Gen. Nankin.) 29 feb. 1836—*Fontes,* n. 4761; S.C. de Prop. Fide (C.P. pro Sin.-Tunkin. Occident.) 27 sept. 1843—*Fontes,* n. 4806.

[20] S.R.C., decr. gen., 30 iun. 1896, n. VI—*Fontes,* n. 6265.

[21] Cf. e.g., Wernz-Vidal, *Ius Matrimoniale,* n. 557; Cappello, *De Matrimonio,* n. 709.

[22] "Benedictio sollemnis regulariter dari et accipi debet eadem die, qua matrimonium contrahitur, nec sine causa rationabili in alium diem forte remotum est differenda." Cappello, *De Matrimonio,* n. 709.

time she requests the blessing. Likewise it is not to be refused to a woman who is being married for the first time, even though it is known that she is not a virgin. The fact that one of the parties of a Catholic marriage still indulges in pagan superstitions is not a reason for refusing the Nuptial Blessing to the marriage.[23]

The reason for the pastor's obligation to administer the Nuptial Blessing to all who legitimately ask for it lies in the fact that the pastor's duty is to administer not only the sacraments but also the sacramentals to all who reasonably ask for them. A pastor who, without any good reason at all, refuses the Nuptial Blessing to those who are legitimately entitled to receive it, makes himself guilty of serious sin if his refusal gives cause for great distress to the contracting parties.[24]

The pastor's second duty in the matter of the Nuptial Blessing, namely, of seeing to it that the married couple receive this bless-

[23] S.C. de Prop. Fide (C.P. pro Sin.-Tunkin, Occident.), 21 iul. 1841, ad 3: "Benedictio quae est in Missali potestne dari illis qui sine illa benedictione iam matrimonio iuncti sunt in primis nuptiis, quando muler iam gravida est, vel iam filios peperit? Item iis qui hic et nunc de praesenti matrimonium contrahunt in primis nuptiis, quando sponsa cognoscitur gravida, vel iam ante matrimonium filios ex fornicatione genuit?" Resp. "Affirmative;" ad 5: "Estne necessarium ut qui iam valide matrimonio iuncti sunt, sint ambo in statu gratiae, ut licite possint recipere benedictionem nuptialem, sive quae in rituali sive quae in Missali est, et quam petunt non ad validitatem eorum matrimonii, sed tantum ne Sacramenti dignitas vilescat, et ut fructus spirituales ex hac benedicione recipiant? In praefato casu sacerdos potestne et debetne illos adhortari ut sese praesentent ad benedictionem nuptialem recipiendam? Quid si una pars est absolutionis capax, alter non?" Resp. "Ad primam partem, convenit. Ad secundam, provisum in prima."—*Fontes,* n. 4791; S.C. de Prop. Fide (C. P. pro Sin.-Tunkin. Occident.), 23 sept. 1843: "Si unus tantum (ex sponsis) vir scilicet aut mulier implicetur superstitionibus, sacerdos poteritne illis dare benedictionem nuptialem in favore partis bene paratae? in contrahendo scilicet, ne (haec) damnum patiatur propter peccatum suae compartis: aut saltem in contiacto (matrimonio), quia tunc non adest periculum profanandi sacramentum: reciperent tantum uberiorem gratiam." Resp. "Iam provisum per responsionem anni 1841." [*Fontes,* n. 4791].—*Fontes,* n. 4803.

[24] Payen, *De Matrimonio,* n. 1868, p. 264, note 3.

ing seems to be clear from canon 1101, § 1, for the words "*parochus curet ut sponsi benedictionem sollemnem accipiant*" seem to connote some sort of obligation on the part of the pastor. Payen observes that this obligation is incumbent not only on the pastor who is actually to assist at the marriage, but that it seems to attach also to all pastors who can validly and licitly assist at the marriage in question.[25] Vlaming notes that a serious reason which prevents the imparting of the Nuptial Blessing frees the pastor from his obligation in this matter.[26]

Canon 1101, § 1, states that the Nuptial Blessing can be imparted to the spouses even after they have been married for some time. In such a case the pastor would have the obligation of imparting the Nuptial Blessing if the couple ask for it. But he seems not to have any obligation of urging the parties who have been married for some time to receive the blessing, for the canon merely says that the blessing *can* be given to such a couple. The word *potest* appears to exclude the presence of any obligation on the part of the pastor.

C—The Minister of the Solemn Blessing

In ordinary cases "the solemn Nuptial Blessing may be given only by the priest who has the right validly and licitly to witness the marriage, or by his delegate." [27] The reason for this prescription of canon 1101 is to be found in canon 462, which enumerates the reserved parochial functions. Among these is the right to assist at marriages and to impart the Nuptial Blessing.[28] Therefore only the local ordinary or the competent pastor of the spouses, especially of the bride, or a priest delegated by either, can impart the Nuptial Blessing, for these alone can validly and licitly assist at the marriage. From a decision of the Holy Office it is evident that the same priest who has said the Nuptial Mass and given the Nuptial Blessing must sprinkle with Holy Water the spouses kneeling at the foot of the altar. It is permissible however for

[25] *De Matrimonio,* n. 1868.
[26] *Praelectiones,* n. 611.
[27] Canon 1101, § 2.
[28] Can. 462. 4°.

the pastor to receive the marriage consent according to the Ritual, and for another priest, with permission of the pastor, to celebrate the Nuptial Mass and impart the Nuptial Blessing.[29] Payen believes that the priest mentioned by canon 1098, 2°, is not to be excluded by canon 1101, 2, from imparting lawfully the Nuptial Blessing.[30]

The ordinary case in which the Nuptial Blessing is imparted immediately after the celebration of the marriage itself has just been discussed. In cases in which the parties have been married according to the ceremonies of the Ritual and then, after a time, ask for the Solemn Blessing, that priest alone can licitly impart it, who could validly and licitly assist at their marriage if they were being married here and now instead of merely requesting the Solemn Blessing. Therefore, if after their marriage the parties change their domicile, the priest who assisted at their marriage is no longer competent to impart the Nuptial Blessing if later on they request it.[31]

D—The Subject of the Solemn Blessing

Unless this blessing is forbidden, all marriages contracted in accordance with the prescriptions of the Church can be blessed with the solemn public official blessing the formulary of which is connected with the Nuptial Mass. The Solemn Blessing can

[29] S.C.S. Off., 1 sept. 1841—Fontes, n. 886. It is disputed whether a priest delegated by the ordinary or the proper local pastor, may, without the permission of the ordinary or the pastor, delegate another priest to impart the Nuptial Blessing, after he himself has assisted at the marriage. Cappello (*De Matrimonio,* n. 710) says that most probably he may do so. This seems to be correct in view of the fact that the authorization for imparting the Nuptial Blessing does not need to be as explicit as that which is required by canon 1096 for the delegation to assist validly at the marriage, since in the conferring of the blessing the question of validity does not arise.

[30] *De Matrimonio,* n. 1869, p. 265, note 3: "Sicut simplicem, ita solemnem, intra Missam, benedictionem dare potest, licet non sit testis auctorizabilis seu ad matrimonii validitatem necessarius." Cf. also *op. cit.,* n. 1825, p. 226, and Cappello, *De Matrimonio,* n. 696.

[31] Aertnys-Damen, *Theologia Moralis,* II, n. 853; Gasparri, *De Matrimonio* (ed. nova), n. 1047.

be forbidden for various reasons: because of the forbidden times;[32] because of a local interdict, either general or particular;[33] because of the presence of certain circumstances attaching to the persons who contract the marriage; because of the specific nature of the contracted marriage itself. The prohibition of the solemn blessing because of the forbidden times will be discussed in the following chapter. The prohibition because of local interdict will also be treated summarily in the same chapter. The other two reasons for the prohibition of the solemn blessing will now be discussed, namely, the circumstances which attach to the persons who contract marriage, and the nature of the contracted marriage itself.

1—The solemn blessing forbidden because of personal circumstances

Because the Nuptial Blessing is given to the spouses themselves, and not to the matrimonial contract, this blessing cannot be imparted unless both parties are present.[34] Therefore it seems that a marriage contracted by proxy cannot receive the solemn blessing. And indeed this opinion is held by Wernz-Vidal,[35] in opposition to Cappello, who says that it is not clear that there is such a prohibition.[36] De Smet asserts that the parties who have

[32] Can. 1108, 2.

[33] Can. 2271, 2°; 2272, § 3, 2°.

[34] S.R.C., *Baionen.*, 27 maii 1911, ad VII: "Utrum ad impertiendam benedictionem nuptialem post tempus feriatum, coniugibus antea matrimonio iunctis, necessaria sit praesentia duorum, vel sufficiat solius sponsae?" Resp. "Affirmative ad primam partem, negative ad secundam." —*Fontes,* n. 6385. Cf. also *Missale Romanum ex decreto Sacrosancti Concilii Tridentini restitutum—S. Pii V Pontificis Maximi iussu editum aliorumque Pontificium cura recognitum—Pii Papae X auctoritate reformatum et Ssmi. D.N. Benedicti XV auctoritate vulgatum* (Romae, Tornaci, Parisiis: Desclee et Socii, 1933), *Additiones et variationes in rubricis Missalis,* II, 2: "Benedictio locum haberi nequit si Sponsi non sint praesentes." The Missal will hereafter be referred to as *Missale Romanum,* and the section mentioned above will be cited as *Addit. et variat.*

[35] *Ius Matrimoniale,* n. 557.

[36] *De Matrimonio,* n. 710, p. 191.

contracted marriage through proxies should be urged to receive the Nuptial Blessing as soon as the occasion presents itself.[37]

The Nuptial Blessing cannot be given to those who have already received it in a previous marriage. If the woman has already received it, it is evident from canon 1143 that the blessing cannot be repeated.[38] This prohibition, as Cappello notes, does not arise from any aversion that the Church has in relation to second marriages, but merely from an established principle of the liturgy of the Church. In as far as the blessing is primarily intended for the woman, it cannot be repeated once she has received it.[39]

Some authors who wrote just prior to the appearance of the new edition of the Ritual in 1925 were of the opinion that the Code in canon 1143 had corrected the previous edition of the Ritual in which it was stated that the blessing could not be repeated if either of the parties had received it before, but in which allowance was made for a contrary custom permitting it to be imparted to the woman, provided that she had not received it before, even though the former marriage of the man had been blessed with the solemn blessing.[40] The new edition of the Ritual, however, has preserved the wording of the former edition. Therefore, in accordance with canon 2, it seems that the wording of the new Ritual has the force of law and that, unless a contrary customs exists, the blessing cannot be repeated if *either* of the parties has received it before.[41] The custom in this country seems

[37] *De Spons. et Mat.*, n. 197, p. 166.

[38] "Mulier cui semel benedictio sollemnis data sit, nequit in subsequentibus nuptiis eam iterum accipere."

[39] *De Matrimonio*, n. 862.

[40] Cf. Wernz-Vidal, *Ius Matrimoniale*, n. 680, p. 821, note 27.

[41] *Rituale Romanum (ad normam Codicis)*, Tit. VII, C. 1, *de sacramento matrimonii*, n. 18: "Caveat autem parochus, ne, quando conjuges in primis nuptiis benedictionem acceperint, eos in secundis benedicat, sive mulier *sive etiam vir* ad secundas nuptias transeat. Sed ubi ea viget consuetudo, ut, si hanc benedictionem vir tantum alias obtinuerit, nuptiae benedicantur, ea servanda est; mulier vero vidua, cui semel benedictio solemnis data sit, nequit in subsequentibus nuptiis eam accipere, etiamsi ejus vir numquam uxorem duxerit." The rubrics of the Missal are in

to be that the only case wherein the blessing is to be denied is the one wherein the woman has previously received it, though the man has never received it.

Some authors are of the opinion that the Nuptial Blessing, because it is a personal blessing, cannot be repeated even though it later becomes evident that the marriage at which it was received was invalid.[42] Consequently the repetition of the blessing would not be allowed when such a marriage was convalidated publicly.[43] Vlaming, however, basing his opinion on the necessity of a valid marriage for the validity of the Nuptial Blessing, holds that, more probably, the blessing may be repeated when an invalid marriage is publicly convalidated.[44] Brennan [45] treating this problem specifically, after careful consideration follows Vlaming's opinion. The writer also agrees with this conclusion.

It is to be noted that in the Appendix to the new Ritual there is a formula for a special blessing, different from the Nuptial Blessing. This may be imparted to a widow who has already received the Nuptial Blessing at a previous marriage.[46] It may also be imparted to a woman who has never been married before, when her marriage occurs during the forbidden times, and when permission has not been obtained from the ordinary to impart the solemn Nuptial Blessing. This special blessing, to be recited immediately after the Ritual ceremonies, cannot be given except by indult from the Holy See, as is indicated from the rubrics which

agreement with the Ritual on this point. Cf. *Addit. et variat.*, II, 2. Cf. also De Smet, *De Spons.* et Mat., n. 198, p. 167, note 4 and Payen, *De Matrimonio*, n. 1873, note 6. The latter observes, however, that while the matter is not entirely clear, it seems that modern practice permits the blessing in every case except that in which the woman has already received the blessing at a previous marriage.

42 Wernz-Vidal, *Ius Matrimoniale*, n. 680, note 25; Payen, *De Matrimonio*, n. 2641.

43 Gasparri, De Matrimonio (ed. 1904), n. 1402.

44 *Praelectiones*, n. 771.

45 *The Simple Convalidation of Marriage*, pp. 95-96.

46 *Rituale Romanum* (*ad normam Codicis*), Appendix, *de matrimonio*, II, *Preces recitandae extra Missam super conjuges ex Apostolicae Sedis indulto quando benedictio nuptialis non permittitur.*

precede this blessing. American bishops have the delegated faculty from the Sacred Congregation of Rites to impart this blessing. They may also subdelegate this faculty to others.[47] Some bishops have subdelegated this power to their priests in the list of the diocesan faculties.[48]

2—The solemn blessing forbidden because of the nature of the contracted marriage.

The Nuptial Blessing is never permitted in mixed marriages, i. e., in marriages between a Catholic and a non-Catholic, whether the latter be baptized or unbaptized. This is evident from canon 1102, § 2, which forbids all sacred rites at such marriages. Even when, to avoid greater evils, the ordinary permits some sacred rites at a mixed marriage, he can never permit the celebration of Mass. Since the nuptial blessing as contained in the Missal can be imparted only during Mass, it follows that this blessing cannot be given at a mixed marriage. Canon 1102 will be treated at length in Chapter VIII of this work.

It seems also that the Nuptial Blessing should be denied in the case wherein even one of the parties of a marriage is numbered among the unworthy Catholics mentioned by canons 1065 and 1066.[49] As Schenk points out, there exists among the authors a divergence of opinion regarding the use of the sacred rites at such marriages. Some say that the silence of the Code regarding the prohibitions of the former law in this matter is to be interpreted as an abrogation of these former prescriptions. Schenk, taking into account the scandal which would be occasioned if such marriages should receive the solemn official blessing of the Church, concludes rightly: "that the decisions antedating the Code must

[47] Bouscaren, *Canon Law Digest* (2 vols. and supplement [1941], Milwaukee: Bruce, 1934-1941), Suppl., p. 33.

[48] Cf. e.g., *Synodus Dioecesana Fargensis Prima, . . . A.D. 1941 habita* (Bruce Milwauchiae, 1941), p. 246, stat. 987, n. 24.

[49] Can. 1066: "Si publicus peccator aut censura notorie innodatus, etc. . . ."

Can. 1065, 1: "Absterreantur quoque fideles a matrimonio contrahendo cum iis qui notories aut catholicam fidem abiecerunt, . . . aut societatibus ab Ecclesia damnatis adscripti sunt.

be used as a norm; that ordinarily the use of sacred rites and the celebration of Mass are prohibited, unless the ordinary sees fit to permit some or all of the rites, and even the celebration of Mass." [50]

E—The Votive Mass pro Sponso et Sponsa

In general the Nuptial Blessing is to be imparted during Mass: during the votive Mass *pro sponso et sponsa* if the rubrics permit it, or during the Mass of the day if the rubrics of the Missal forbid the votive Mass. During the forbidden times the Nuptial Blessing cannot be imparted even during the Mass of the day without the permission of the ordinary.

1—The Nuptial Blessing to be given during Mass

It is clear from a number of responses of the Sacred Congregations and from the rubrics of the Missal that, except by apostolic indult, the Nuptial Blessing cannot be given outside of Mass.[51] A formula for imparting the Nuptial Blessing outside of Mass is found in the appendix to the Ritual. Though this formula differs from the Nuptial Blessing as found in the votive Nuptial Mass, it is clear from its title as compared with that of the prayers found in the appendix under II, and also from the rubrics prefixed to both I and II of the appendix, that it is a true Nuptial Blessing, a public official blessing of the Church. Like the prayers under II, this Nuptial Blessing cannot be imparted without an apostolic indult.[52] The ordinaries of this country have this faculty in their quinquennial faculties.[53] They also have the power of

[50] Schenk, *Mixed Religion and Disparity of Cult,* pp. 276-278.

[51] S.C.S. Off., 31 aug. 1881—*Fontes,* n. 1071; S.R.C., *Limburgen.,* 23 iun 1853, ad 1 et 2—*Fontes,* n. 5967; S.R.C., *Romana,* 9 maii 1893—*Fontes,* n. 6226; S.R.C., decr. gen., 30 iun. 1896, n. VI—*Fontes,* n. 6265; S.R.C., *Belemen. de Para,* 12 febu. 1909—*Fontes,* n. 6372; *Missale Romanum, addit. et variat.,* II, 2.

[52] *Rituale Romanum (ad normam Codicis),* Appendix, *de matrimonio,* I: *Benedictio nuptialis extra Missam danda ex Apostolico indulto quando Missa non dicitur.*

[53] Bouscaren, *Canon Law Digest,* Supplement 1941, p. 33.

subdelegating this faculty, and some bishops have done so in the list of diocesan faculties.[54]

The votive Mass *pro sponso et sponsa* is so intimately connected with the Nuptial Blessing found in the Missal that it cannot be said unless the blessing is imparted. If Mass is said for parties who cannot receive the Nuptial Blessing, it must be the Mass of the day or a votive Mass other than the Nuptial Mass. On the other hand, the votive Mass *pro sponso et sponsa* must be said whenever the rubrics permit it, if the solemn blessing is given. It is not optional to choose either the Nuptial Mass or the mass of the day.[55] If the priest who is to give the solemn blessing receives no stipend from the parties for the Mass, nevertheless this is not a reason for omitting the Nuptial Mass, and for saying the Mass of the day. He must say the Nuptial Mass. He is free to apply it for the parties, but he is also free to apply it for an intention connected with a stipend which he has received.[56]

2—Days on which the Nuptial Mass is permitted.

Though the Nuptial Mass is a private votive Mass, it is not subject to the usual regulations for private votive Masses, but is regulated by the "special rubric" mentioned by canon 1101, § 1. This rubric is found immediately at the head of the Nuptial Mass; it is also printed in the section entitled *"Additiones et variationes in rubricis missalis"* as found in front of the Missal.[57] Therefore it is permitted on many more days than the ordinary private votive Masses. It is prohibited on the following days.

a. On all Sundays and holy days of obligation (the ten holy days listed in canon 1247, § 1), and also on the suppressed holy days.[58]

[54] Cf., e.g., *Synodus Fargensis Prima*, p. 246, stat. 987, n. 24.

[55] Cf. the rubrics preceding the *Missa pro sponso et sponsa;* also S.R.C., decr. gen. 30 iun. 1896, n. VI—*Fontes,* n. 6265.

[56] S.C.S. Off., 1 sept. 1841, n. 3—*Fontes,* n. 886; S.C. de Prop. Fide (C.P. pro Sin.-Tunkin. Orient.), 10 ian. 1837—*Fontes,* n. 4764.

[57] *Addit. et variat.*, II, *De missis votivis;* n. 1 treats of private votive Masses in general, n. 2 of the Nuptial Mass.

[58] A list of the suppressed feasts is given in the *AAS,* XII (1920),

b. On doubles of the first or second class.

c. During privileged octaves of the first (Easter and Pentecost) and second order (Epiphany and Corpus Christi).

d. On privileged ferias, i. e., Ash Wednesday, and the Monday, Tuesday and Wednesday of Holy Week (the last three days of Holy Week are doubles of the first class), and on privileged vigils (privileged vigils of the first class are those of Christmas and Pentecost, of the second class is the vigil of Epiphany).

Not only the Nuptial Mass but also the Nuptial Blessing is forbidden on the day of the Commemoration of the Faithful Departed.[59] The same is true if there is only one Mass in the church and that is a funeral Mass.[60] The Nuptial Mass may not be said when there is only one parish Mass on the rogation days and the procession follows, because if the procession takes place the rogation Mass must be said. In this case, however, the Nuptial Mass may be commemorated and the nuptial blessing given.[61]

Finally the Nuptial Mass and Blessing are forbidden during the *tempus clausum,* as outlined in canon 1108, § 2. If the ordinary permits the Nuptial Blessing, then the Nuptial Mass or the Mass of the day is to be said, according as the day is one of the days on which the Nuptial Mass is or is not permitted. The reader is referred to the list above.

42-43: the Monday and Tuesday following Easter and Pentecost, the Feast of the Finding of the Holy Cross, the Purification, the Annunciation, the Nativity of our Lady, the Dedication of St. Michael the Archangel, the Nativity of St. John the Baptist, the Feasts of the Apostles,—i.e., St. Andrew, St. James, St. John, St. Thomas, Sts. Philip and James, St. Bartholomew, St. Matthew, Sts. Simon and Jude, St. Matthias,—the Feast of St. Stephen Protomartyr, the Feast of the Holy Innocents, the Feast of St. Lawrence Martyr, the Feast of St. Silvester Pope, the Feast of St. Anne, the Patronal Feast of a country, the Feast of the Patron of a locality. In practice, however, as far as the nuptial mass is concerned, the Feast of St. Sylvester is the only one to be remembered, since all of the other supressed feasts are doubles of the first or second class, and on such doubles the nuptial mass is prohibited.

59 Cf. the rubrics of the *Missa pro sponso et sponsa.*

60 S.C.S. Off., 1 sept. 1841, n. 6—*Fontes,* n. 886.

61 S.R.C., *Marsorum,* 12 nov. 1831—*Decr. Auth.,* n. 2682, ad 35.

3—The rite in which the Nuptial Mass is to be said.

The Nuptial Mass, since it is a private votive Mass, follows the rubrics prescribed for private votive Masses, namely, it is to be said without *Gloria* and *Credo;* the orations, outside of Passion Week, are to be three in number, the first being that of the Nuptial Mass, the second and third those of the day; the *Benedicamus Domino* is said, and the last gospel is that of St. John, unless the rubrics demand a special gospel. The color of the vestments is white.[62] If the Nuptial Mass is said on a feast of double rite, no orations *de tempore* are to be added. The oration of the Nuptial Mass is followed by the oration of the double feast, and any other commemorations which would be made if the Mass of the double feast itself were said.[63]

F—*The Mass of the Day*

When the "special rubric" of the votive Mass *pro sponso et sponsa* prohibits the celebration of the Nuptial Mass, without at the same time forbidding the imparting of the Nuptial Blessing, the Mass of the day is to be said, and the Nuptial Blessing (the three orations *Propitiare, Domine, Deus, qui potestate,* and *Deus Abraham*) is to be inserted in the Mass of the day at the same points at which it is imparted in the Nuptial Mass.[64] Furthermore a commemoration of the votive Mass *pro sponso et sponsa* is to be made, namely the collect *Exaudi nos,* the secret *Suscipe,* and the post-communion *Quaesumus,* are to be inserted after the oration, secret and post-communion respectively of the Mass of the day. These prayers are to be joined to the prayers of the Mass of the day

[62] S.R.C., decr. gen., 30 iun. 1896, n. VI—*Fontes,* n. 6265; *Missale Romanum, addit. et variat.,* II, *de missis votivis.*

[63] S.R.C., Dubia, 24 maii 1912, ad VII: "In Missis pro Sponsis, sicut in aliis Missis votivis ex privilegio celebratis, in duplicibus adiungendane est tertia oratio?" Resp. "Negative ."—*AAS,* IV (1912), 419-420.

[64] If the blessing is not given during the forbidden times, and the spouses request it afterwards, a day does not have to be chosen on which the votive Mass *pro sponso et sponsa* must be said. The blessing can be imparted during the Mass of the day in the manner described above. Cf. S.R.C., *Baionen.,* 27 maii 1911, ad VI—*Fontes,* n. 6385.

under one conclusion in all cases, even on first class feasts and feast which exclude a second oration, not excluding the Feasts of Easter and Christmas, if permission is given to impart the Nuptial Blessing on these two latter feasts which occur during the forbidden times.[65]

[65] Cf. the rubric before the Introit of the *Missa pro sponso et sponsa*, and *Rituale Romanum (ad normam Codicis), addit. et variat.*, II, n. 2. Formerly the rule was that the oration of the Nuptial Mass was to be added under a separate conclusion. Cf. S.R.C., decr. gen., 30 iun. 1896, n. VI—*Fontes*, n. 6265. In 1918 the Sacred Congregation of Rites, after hearing from the Code Commission, answered a query in this matter by saying that on the Feasts of Easter and Christmas, if permission had been given for the Nuptial Blessing, the oration of the Nuptial Mass was to be added to the orations of these feasts under one conclusion. This left some doubt as to whether this applied only to Easter and Christmas, or whether the oration of the Nuptial Mass, whenever it was added to the oration of the day, was to be added under one conclusion. Cf. "Some recent decisions concerning the Nuptial Blessing," *Irish Eccesliastical Record*, 5th series, XII (1918), 419-421. The new edition of the Missal in 1925 removed all doubt in the matter. In the section *Additiones et Variationes in rubricis missalis*, II, n. 2, it was clearly stated that on those days on which the Nuptial Mass could not be said, but on which the blessing was permitted, the mass of the day was to be said and the Nuptial Mass was to be commemorated always under one conclusion.

CHAPTER VI

THE TIME FOR THE CELEBRATION OF MARRIAGE

Canon 1108

§ 1. Matrimonium quolibet anni tempore contrahi potest.

§ 2. Sollemnis tantum nuptiarum benedictio vetatur a prima dominica Adventus usque ad diem Nativitatis inclusive, et a feria IV Cinerum usque ad dominicam Paschatis inclusive.

§ 3. Ordinarii tamen locorum possunt, salvis legibus liturgicis, etiam praedictis temporibus eam permittere ex iusta causa, monitis sponsis ut a nimia pompa abstineant.

Canon 1108 sets forth in a few lines the present discipline regarding the ancient institute of forbidden times. The Church, while keeping in mind the purpose for which the legislation on forbidden times was instituted,[1] has mitigated considerably the legislation in this regard. Not only is the length of the times themselves shortened, but local ordinaries are empowered, under certain conditions, to grant permission for the Nuptial Blessing during the forbidden times. This latter provision is new with the Code, never having existed in the former law. It is contained in paragraph three of the canon quoted above, and was among the provisions which became effective in advance of the Code.[2]

The ceremonies of the Roman Ritual (or approved diocesan

[1] I.e., that the solemnities of marriage might not interfere with the penitential spirit of certain times of the year (in the present law, Lent and Advent), or with the reception of the sacraments and the contemplation of the great mysteries of religion on certain feasts (in the Code, the Feasts of Christmas and Easter). Cf. *supra*, pp. 13-14 De Smet notes, however, that these reasons had more significance in ancient times when the exchange of marital consent was often made privately and without solemnity, followed later by the marriage solemnized *in facie Ecclesiae* with the Nuptial Mass and Blessing, and the secular festivities which followed. Cf. De Smet, *De Spons. et Mat.*, p. 169, note 1.

[2] Secret. Stat., 20 aug. 1917—*AAS*, IX (1917), 475.

ritual) must be used for the marriage rite, except in mixed marriages and in cases of urgent necessity. Further, the rites of the Ritual, along with the exchange of consent, may be termed the simple Nuptial Blessing, in contradistinction to the solemn Nuptial Blessing which is imparted only during Mass.[3] Therefore one may say in general that paragraph one of canon 1108 treats of the time for the simple or ritual blessing, when it states that marriage may be contracted at any time of the year. Paragraphs two and three treat of the time for the solemn blessing, the former stating the times during which it is forbidden, the latter laying down the conditions under which the local ordinary may permit the solemn blessing during the forbidden times. The first article of this chapter, then, will discuss the time for the simple blessing, and the second will treat of the time for the solemn or Nuptial Blessing properly so called. In each article a resumé of the pre-Code law will be given, in order that the changes introduced by the Code may be more apparent.

Article I—The Time For The Simple Blessing

In the universal legislation of the Church which was in force before 1918 there was no prohibition of the celebration of marriage with the attendant ceremonies of the Ritual. Then, as in the Code, the principle was that marriage could be contracted lawfully at any time of the year.[4] This was the common law of the Church, but it did not exclude a more rigorous discipline sanctioned by particular law or custom in some dioceses, according to which even the simple celebration of marriage was prohibited during the closed time, unless a dispensation had been obtained from the ordinary.[5] Such laws or customs were sanctioned by the Council of Trent when it stated its wish that any praiseworthy customs in the matter of marriage, over and above the general law, were to be retained.[6]

[3] Cf. *supra*, pp. 10-12, 62-63.

[4] C. 4, X, *de feriis* II, 9; cf. also *supra*, pp. 25-28.

[5] Cf. *supra*, pp. 24-25.

[6] Sess. XXIV, *de ref. matrim.*, c. 1.

The Code in paragraph one has retained the principle that marriage may be celebrated at any time of the year. Therefore particular laws opposed to the ruling of this canon are automatically abrogated,[7] as also are particular customs, unless they are century-old or immemorable, and the ordinary cannot prudently suppress them.[8] In order, then, to discover which customs or laws are opposed to canon 1108, § 1, an inquiry must be made into the true meaning of this paragraph. From such an investigation certain conclusions will be drawn regarding three points. 1. Legislation or custom forbidding the marriage ceremony itself during Lent or Advent. 2. Legislation or custom prohibiting marriage in the afternoon or evening. 3. Legislation or custom forbidding marriage on certain days of the year, e. g., on Sundays or Holy Days.

1. The sense of paragraph one of the canon, if taken in opposition to paragraph two, is at least the following: "Marriage can be celebrated at any time of the year, even during those times which, according to paragraph two, forbid the solemn Nuptial Blessing."[9] In the new law the notion of forbidden times does not exclude the simple celebration of marriage, but only its solemn celebration. Hence even during the forbidden times the spouses have a right to the ceremonies and the blessing of the Ritual.[10]

Therefore according to the principle enunciated in n. 1 of canon 6, diocesan or provincial laws which prohibit the simple celebration of marriage during the forbidden times are suppressed by § 1 of canon 1108. With regard to customs in this matter, the

[7] Can. 6, 1°: "Les quaelibet, sive universales sive particulares, praescriptis huius Codicis oppositae, abrogantur, nisi de particularibus legibus aliud expresse caveatur."

[8] Can. 5: "Vigens in praesens contra horum statuta canonum consuetudines sive universales sive particulares, si quidem ipsis canonibus expresse *reprobentur,* tanquan iuris corruptelae corrigantur, licet sint immemorabiles, neve sinantur in posterum reviviscere; aliae, quae quidem centenariae sint et immemorabiles, tolerari poterunt, si Ordinarii pro locorum ac personarum adiunctis existiment eas prudenter submoveri non posse; ceterae suppressae habeantur, nisi expresse Codex aliud caveat."

[9] Payen, *De Matrimonio,* n. 1951; Vlaming, *Praelectiones,* n. 613.

[10] Chelodi, *Ius Matrimoniale,* n. 145.

principle of canon 5 is to be applied. Hence a custom which forbids the celebration of marriage during the forbidden times is suppressed, unless it be century-old or immemorable. Even in this case the ordinary has the obligation of suppressing it, unless in his prudence he forsees that this cannot be done. In fact any custom in this regard, regardless of its antiquity, would seem to be a *corruptela iuris,* and hence to be suppressed. For such a custom would have the force of a prohibitive impediment to the celebration of marriage during the closed time, and canon 1041 expressly reprobates any custom introducing a new impediment contrary to the Code.[11] Moreover, as De Smet notes, it is difficult to see how such a custom could not be prudently eliminated by the bishop. He recounts that the Bishop of Bruges in a prosynodal congregation issued a decree suppressing a diocesan statute which forbade the simple celebration of marriage during the closed times.[12] Vermeersch-Creusen [13] and Gougnard [14] mention that the Fourth Council of Malines (1920) suppressed an immemorable custom by virtue of which, in Belgium, it was forbidden to contract marriage during the closed times, without a dispensation from the ordinary. Gougnard notes, however, that the Council's decree contained a *votum* that the faithful should be deterred (*avertantur fideles ne nuptias ineant*) from contracting marriage on ember days and other days of abstinence. Whether or not such a prescription would be contrary to canon 1108, § 1, will be seen later. Suffice it to say now that any law or custom

[11] Can. 1041: "Consuetudo novum impedimentum inducens aut impedimentis existentibus contraria reprobatur:" Cf. De Smet, *De Spons. et Mat., n.* 199, p. 168, note 1. Cf. also O'Donnell, "Sections of the New Code in Force," *Irish Ecclesiastical Record,* 5th series, X (1917), 353-366, especially IV, "Forbidden times of marriage," 365-366; and Wernz-Vidal, *Ius Matrimoniale,* n. 575, p. 674, note 19.

[12] *De Spons. et Mat.,* n. 199, p. 168, note 1.

[13] *Epitome Iuris Canonici* (3 vols. [Vol. I, 6. ed., Vols. II & III, 5. ed.], Mechliniae-Romae: H. Dessain, 1934-1937), II, n. 411. This work will hereafter be cited as *Epitome.*

[14] *Tractatus de Matrimonio* (7. ed., Mechliniae: H. Dessain, 1931), p. 180.

forbidding marriage during Lent or Advent is opposed to canon 1108, § 1, and if a law, is to be abrogated, if a custom, is to be suppressed.

2. Regarding the time of the day at which marriage may be celebrated the canon in question says nothing. Therefore it may be concluded that, according to the general law, there is nothing to prevent the celebration of marriage at any hour of the day or night.[15] But this does not seem to warrant such an interpretation of canon 1108, § 1, as would say that it permits marriage at any hour even when there is a particular law limiting the time for the celebration of marriage.[16] The Code does not say clearly that marriages are permitted at any hour, but merely states that marriage may be celebrated at any time (or day) of the year.[17] Hence, as Cappello observes, it is fully within the bishop's power to prohibit, for a good reason, evening weddings in particular cases. "But," the same author continues, "can he do so by a general statute?" He replies that some deny him this power, because, as they say, the words *quolibet anni tempore* of canon 1108, § 1, can be understood not only of the day but of the hours of the day also, since these words are altogether general in character. Against this argument he opposes canon 1171, which allows the ordinary to fix the hours for ceremonies and sacred rites for a just cause.[18] He also draws an argument from canon 23 which says that, when there is a doubt as to the revocation

[15] Chelodi, *Ius Matrimoniale*, n. 145; Cappello, *De Matrimonio*, n. 726; Rossi, *De Matrimonii Celebratione*, n. 70; Fanfani *(De Iure Parochorum* [2. ed., Taurini-Romae: Marietti, 1936], n. 329) in quoting the text of canon 1108, § 1, adds in brackets the words *et qualibet hora diei.*

[16] Payen, *De Matrimonio*, n. 1951. Cf. also "Notes and Queries," *Irish Ecclesiastical Record*, 5th series, XXXIII (1929), 61.

[17] Ayrinhac, *Marriage Legislation in the New Code of Cannon Law* (new, rev. ed., New York: Benziger Bros., 1938), n. 269. To be quoted hereafter as *Marriage Legislation.*

[18] "In sacra aede legitime dedicata omnes ecclesiastici ritus perfici possunt, salvis iuribus paroecialibus, privilegiis et legitimis consuetudinibus; Ordinarius autem, praesertim horas sacrorum rituum, potest, iusta de causa, praefinire, dummodo ne agatur de ecclesia quae ad religionem exemptam pertineat, firmo praescripto can. 609, § 3."

of a pre-existing law, its revocation is not to be presumed, but it is to be reconciled as far as possible with the existing law.[19] Now, as Wernz-Vidal observe, many provincial councils before the Code had regulations forbidding afternoon or evening weddings, and these regulations were approved by Rome, which usually corrects whatever is too strict or too lax in conciliar legislation. Such legislation and the legislation of diocesan synods would seem still to be in force, since it is not against the law of the Code, but over and above its prescriptions.[20]

Gasparri says that a law which forbids evening or afternoon weddings is a sound one, because experience teaches that when marriages take place in the evening, it often happens that, among untutored people, the bridal party is almost inebriated when it arrives at the church. He alleges as a further reason that if evening weddings are permitted promiscuously, the laudable and ancient custom of blessing the marriage during Mass would disappear altogether.[21]

Cappello observes that the opinion which favors the validity of diocesan or provincial laws forbidding afternoon or evening weddings is the more probable one.[22] Indeed, so great is the weight of extrinsic authority in favor of this opinion that there would seem to be no authority for the other opinion. Cappello, Chelodi, Gasparri, Payen, Rossi, Vlaming, Wernz-Vidal and Ayrinhac, all hold this opinion.

3. There is not the same unanimity of opinion, however, among the authors as to the validity of legislation forbidding marriages on certain days, e. g., on Sundays or Holy Days. It is a matter of dispute whether the words *quolibet anni tempore* expressly permit the celebration of marriage on any day whatsoever, or if they merely mean that at no time of the year, even if it be in

[19] "In dubio revocatio legis praeexsistentis non praesumitur, sed leges posteriores ad priores trahendae sunt et his, quantum fieri possit, conciliandae." Cf. Cappello, *De Matrimonio*, n. 726, p. 208.

[20] Wernz-Vidal, *Ius Matrimoniale*, n. 577, and notes 21 and 22; Chelodi, *Ius Matrimoniale*, n. 145.

[21] *De Matrimonio* (ed. nova), n. 1062.

[22] *De Matrimonio*, n. 726.

Article II—The Time For The Solemn Blessing

A—*The Former Law*

As in the previous article, so here also a brief resumé of the former law will help the reader to obtain a fuller understanding of the law of the Code. In this connection the following points will be examined. 1. The content of the legal prohibition. 2. The extent of the forbidden times. 3. The inability of the bishop to dispense from the law.[31]

1. The Council of Trent commanded that the "ancient prohibitions of nuptial solemnities" be faithfully observed by all the faithful.[32] The old edition of the ritual (a new *editio typica* was published in 1925) sets forth these prohibited solemnities: the solemn Nuptial Blessing, the escorting of the bride to the home of her husband (*traductio sponsae*), and the wedding banquet.[33] The prohibition against the Nuptial Blessing was a serious one. Pastors or spouses who violated it were guilty of serious sin. The two other prohibitions were not of such a serious nature, unless the violation of them gave scandal or was so flagrant as to be altogether out of keeping with the spirit of the forbidden times.[34]

2. According to the law of the Council of Trent "these ancient prohibitions of nuptial solemnities" were forbidden from the first Sunday of Advent until the Feast of the Epiphany inclusively, and from the first Sunday of Lent until Low Sunday inclusively.[35] The prohibition began at midnight preceding the first day, and ended at midnight following the last day of the periods mentioned. These were the forbidden times from the Council of Trent to the Code.[36]

3. It has been seen in the historical part of this work that be-

[31] For a more complete exposition of the pre-Code law, i.e., the law of the Council of Trent, cf. pp. 21-35 *supra*.

[32] Sess. XXIV, *de ref. matrim.*, c. 10.

[33] *Rituale Romanum*, Tit. VII, *De Sacramento Matrimonii*, C. I, n. 16.

[34] Sanchez, *De Matrimonio*, Lib. VII, disp. 7, n. 3, also nn. 16, 18.

[35] Sess. XXIV, *de ref. matrim.*, c. 10.

[36] Before the time of the Council of Trent there were three forbidden periods. Cf. p. 19 *supra*.

fore the Code there was, in many dioceses, a prohibition against even the simple celebration of marriage during Lent and Advent, unless a dispensation had been obtained from the bishop. Even in the case wherein the bishop granted such a permission he could not give permission for the Nuptial Mass and Blessing. Such a permission could only be given by the Holy See, which rarely, if ever, granted it.[37]

In the following section on the present law it will be found that, of the three points of the old law just treated, two of them, namely, the things forbidden and the extent of the times themselves, were changed to some extent by the Code. The latter point, the incompetency of the bishop to permit the Nuptial Blessing, was abrogated altogether by the Code.

B—*The Law of the Code*

In this section on the new law, analogously to the treatment of the former law, the following points will be considered. 1. The content of the legal prohibition. 2. The extent of the forbidden times. 3. The power of the local ordinary to dispense.

1—The Content of the Legal Prohibition

From paragraph two of canon 1108 it is certain that the Nuptial Blessing is forbidden: *sollemnis tantum nuptiarum benedictio vetatur.* In other words, the celebration of matrimony and the simple blessing of the Ritual are not forbidden, but only the solemn Nuptial Blessing, which is contained in the Missal in the votive Mass *pro sponso et sponsa.* Therefore there is nothing to prevent the parties from being married before Mass with the Ritual ceremonies, but the Mass which follows cannot be the Nuptial Mass, nor can a commemoration of the Nuptial Mass be made, neither can the Nuptial Blessing be imparted.[38]

In the former law the prohibition of the solemn blessing and of the Nuptial Mass was always considered a serious one.[39] This

[37] Cf. *supra*, pp. 34-35.

[38] S.R.C., *Montis Pessulani,* 31 aug. 1938—*Fontes*, n. 5899.

[39] Sanchez, *De Matrimonio,* Lib. VII, disp. 7, n. 9.

is shown by the fact that, up to the Code, the bishops never had the power of permitting this blessing and Mass during the closed time. Wernz-Vidal still hold to the serious nature of the prohibition even after the Code.[40] Some authors, however, e. g., Vlaming, arguing from the fact that the bishop can now dispense from the prohibition, state that it seems difficult to be able to regard the obligation as a serious one.[41] Payen, however, says that most probably there is a serious obligation,[42] and this seems to the writer to be the better opinion.

While it is clear that the Nuptial Blessing and the Nuptial Mass are forbidden, the matter is not equally clear regarding the other two items included among the *sollemnitates nuptiarum* under the former law, namely, the escorting of the bride in solemn procession to the home of her husband (*traductio in domum*) and the sumptuous wedding banquet (*nuptiale convivium*).[43] Most authors, however, hold that the only thing forbidden by the Code is the solemn Nuptial Blessing along with the Nuptial Mass. In fact, De Smet seems to stand alone in his contention that the *traductio in domum* and the *nuptiale convivium* are also interdicted during the forbidden times.[44] He bases his argument on n. 4 of canon 6 [45] and on canon 2.[46] He claims also that the wording of § 3 of canon 1108 favors his opinion. That paragraph states that when the solemn blessing is permitted the *spouses* are warned to avoid excessive display. He argues that if it were merely a question of religious solemnity the word *parochi* would be used instead of *sponsi*. But the spouses are the ones who can moderate *secular display*. As a further argument he adduces the fact that the alphabetical index uses the words *sollemnitates nup-*

40 *Ius Matrimoniale,* n. 575.

41 *Praelectiones,* n. 614.

42 *De Matrimonio,* n. 1953.

43 Cf. Conc. Trident., sess. XXIV, *de ref. matrim.,* c. 10; also *Rituale Romanum,* Tit. VII, *De Sacramento Matrimonii,* C. I, n. 16.

44 *De Spons. et Mat.,* n. 199, and note 4.

45 Can. 6, 4°: "In dubio num aliquod canonum praescriptum cum veteri iure discrepet, a veteri iure non est recendum."

46 For the text of canon 2 cf. *supra,* p. 63.

tiarum, i. e., the words which were used in the former law to designate not only the Nuptial Blessing but also the *traductio in domum* and the wedding banquet. Vermeersch-Creusen note that the argument deduced from the alphabetical index is not a very strong one. They add, further, that the force of the wording of the Code is not to be extended over much to make it agree with the old law.[47]

Vlaming subscribes to the opinion which is contrary to De Smet's, and bases his argument on the silence of the Code regarding the *traductio in domum* and the wedding banquet. If the legislator had intended to include these he would have used the wording of the old law, viz., *sollemnitates nuptiarum.* Therefore the Code wishes to forbid only that pomp, liturgical or quasi-liturgical, which is, as it were, identified with the Nuptial Blessing.[48]

Cappello also rejects De Smet's opinion, calling it improbable in view of the wording of § 2 and § 3, in which there is question only of the Nuptial Blessing, and in which the spouses are warned merely to avoid *excessive* display.[49] Gasparri,[50] Wernz-Vidal,[51] Blat,[52] De Becker,[53] and Gougnard,[54] all favor the opinion that only the solemn Nuptial Blessing is forbidden. The latter adds that the controversy between Cappello and De Smet has not much practical importance.[55] And indeed the *traductio in domum* as it was understood in the old law, namely, the solemn induction of the bride into the home of the bridegroom, is not customary now-

[47] *Epitome,* II, n. 412, note 1.

[48] *Praelectiones,* n. 613, p. 221 and p. 222, note 1.

[49] *De Matrimonio,* n. 726, p. 208, note 2.

[50] *De Matrimonio* (ed. nova), n. 1061.

[51] *Ius Matrimoniale,* n. 575.

[52] *Commentarium Textus Codicis Iuris Canonici* (5 vols. in 7, Vol. III, Pars I [*De Sacramentis*], 2. ed., Romae: Ex typographia Ponitficia in Instituto Pii, 1924), n. 515.

[53] *De Matrimonio Praelectiones Canonicae* (editio nova ad tramites codicis iuris canonici accomodata, Louvain: Fr. Ceuterick, 1931, p. 200. Hereafter *De Matrimonio* (ed. nova).

[54] *De Matrimonio,* p. 180.

[55] *Ibidem,* note 1.

adays, as Augustine notes, except in Slavic countries.[56] And, as Gasparri observes, the wedding banquet has become almost a natural sequel to the wedding ceremony.[57]

The opinion of all these authors that the solemn Nuptial Blessing alone is forbidden during the closed time is further strengthened by the fact that in the new Ritual the words *sollemnitates nuptiarum* are omitted, and canon 1108 is quoted in its entirety.[58]

2.—The Extent of the Forbidden Times

The new law has shortened the length of the forbidden times by a few weeks. Now the solemn Nuptial Blessing and the Nuptial Mass are forbidden only from the first Sunday of Advent up to Christmas day inclusively, and from the first Sunday of Lent up to Easter Sunday inclusively. The beginning and end of these seasons are to be reckoned according to canon 32, § 1, so that the closed times begin on midnight of Saturday before the first Sunday of Advent, and of the Saturday before the first Sunday of Lent, and close at midnight of Christmas day and of Easter Sunday.[59]

3.—The Power Granted to the Ordinary for Dispensing

As has already been observed § 3 of canon 1108 gives to local ordinaries a power which they did not have in pre-Code law: "The local ordinaries may permit the solemn Nuptial Blessing for a good reason, subject to the laws of the sacred liturgy, but they must admonish the parties to refrain from too much pomp." The local ordinary, hence also the vicar-general and all those who

[56] *A Commentary on the New Code of Canon Law* (8 vols., Vol. V, *Marriage Law, Matrimonial Trials*, 5. ed., St. Louis, Mo.: B. Herder Book Co., 1935), p. 320. Hereafter this volume will be cited as *Marriage Law*.

[57] *De Matrimonio*, (ed. nova), n. 1061.

[58] *Rituale Romanum (ad normam Codicis)*, Tit. VII, *De Sacramento Matrimonii*, C. I, n. 19; cf. also Rossi, "L'Istituto del Matrimonio in Italia dopo il Concordato Lateranense. (Continuazione),"—*Perfice Munus*, VII (1932), 838.

[59] Can. 32, § 1: "Dies constat 24 horis continuo supputandis a media nocte. . . ."

are mentioned in canon 198 as local ordinaries,[60] can permit, under the conditions stated in canon 1108, § 3, the solemn Nuptial Blessing to be imparted at a marriage which is to be contracted during the forbidden times. But if a marriage is contracted immediately before the closed time begins, the ordinary may not permit the blessing to be supplied during the closed time.[61] That the ordinary may grant this permission two conditions are to be fulfilled: the rules of the liturgy must be observed, and there must be a good cause for granting the permission.

Regarding the observance of the rules of the liturgy the following points are to be noted. The Nuptial Blessing cannot be given outside of Mass except by apostolic indult.[62] Furthermore if the rules of liturgy permit the votive Nuptial Mass, this mass must be said and the nuptial blessing imparted during it. On the days, however, on which the Mass *pro sponso et sponsa* is not permitted, the Mass of the day is to be said with a commemoration of the Nuptial Mass under one conclusion; and the special prayers of the Nuptial Blessing are to be said at those points in the Holy Sacrifice which are designated by the rubrics of the *Missa pro sponso et sponsa.*[63]

Regarding the cause for the dispensation from the law of § 2, it is to be held that any good cause suffices. The Code says *causa iusta* and not *causa gravis.* The Church wishes that all who are

[60] Can. 198, § 1: "In iure nomine *Ordinarii* intelliguntur, nisi quis expresse excipiatur, praeter Romanum Pontificem, pro suo quisque territorio Episcopus residentialis, Abbas vel Praelatus *nullius* eorumque Vicarius Generalis, Administrator, Vicarius et Praefectus Apostolicus, itemque ii qui praedictis deficientibus interim ex iuris praescripto aut ex probatis constitutionibus succedunt in regimine, pro suis vero subditis Superiores maiores in religionibus clericalibus exemptis."

§ 2: "Nomine autem *Ordinarii loci* seu *locorum* veniunt omnes recensiti, exceptis Superioribus religiosis."

[61] Payen, *De Matrimonio,* n. 1953, p. 321 (end of page).

[62] The American bishops, according to their quinquennial faculties, have the delegated faculty from the Sacred Congregation of Rites of blessing marriages outside of mass with the formula of the Nuptial Blessing found in the appendix of the new Ritual. Cf. *supra* p. 79.

[63] For the complete discussion of these liturgical laws the reader is referred to Chapter V, *supra,* pp. 79-83.

about to contract marriage should receive the Nuptial Blessing if they are capable of receiving it, and she knows from experience that those who do not receive it on the occasion of their marriage will not ordinarily return later to obtain it. This is the reason for the ease with which the dispensation may be granted in virtue of § 3. With this taken into account, the fact that the spouses wish to receive the Nuptial Blessing will be a good reason for granting the dispensation, provided that they cannot postpone their marriage without inconvenience until after the closed time.[64] As Payen notes, if the permission is asked for there will usually be a sufficient cause for granting it.[65]

When the bishop grants the dispensation which is made available by § 3, he is told to admonish the parties to avoid all lavish pomp. Rossi calls attention to the fact that the word *monita* shows that there is a question of a warning and not of a strict precept. He also calls attention to the word *nimia*; hence it is not all pomp or display that is interdicted, but only that which is excessive.[66] But in the concrete, what exactly is meant by lavish pomp? Authors differ in the matter, some claiming that the canon speaks of excess only in the liturgical or quasi-liturgical aspect of the celebration of marriage, others applying the words *nimia pompa* not only to the Nuptial Blessing and the circumstances which accompany it, but also to any kind of excessive display. Thus Vermeersch-Creusen say that the wedding party should not be very numerous, their dress should not be lavish, the decoration of the church should be moderate.[67] De Becker says approximately the same thing.[68] Rossi says the words *nimia pompa* apply to the

[64] Cf. "Quelle est la portée du canon 1108?" *L'Ami du Clergé,* XLVI (1929), 10-11.

[65] *De Matrimonio,* n. 1953, p. 322. Augustine, *Marriage Law,* says on p. 320: "A sufficient reason would be if the pastor visits a mission only at rare intervals or the couple lives at a great distance from church; also the sudden departure of a soldier for the barracks or battlefield."

[66] *De Matrimonii Celebratione,* n. 70; cf. also Rossi, "L'Istituto del Matrimonio in Italia dopo il Concordato Lateranense. (continuazione),"—*Perfice Munus,* VII (1932), 838.

[67] *Epitome,* II, n. 412.

[68] *De Matrimonio* (ed. nova), p. 199.

religious rites alone.[69] Payen,[70] Wernz-Vidal[71] and Cappello,[72] however, apply the words *nimia pompa* not only to what takes place in church but also to what follows the wedding, e. g., the banquet, the dance, in a word any secular celebration that is of an excessive nature.

A writer in the Australasian Catholic Record gives an interesting statement in this connection. "*Nimia pompa* must be interpreted by local standards. It is certainly to be advised that the incongruity of the celebration with the Church's mind should be shown forth by the retention of the sombre and penitential appearance of altar and sanctuary. Let the organ be kept in sorrowful silence."[73] Since the Church grants the spouses the privilege of receiving the Nuptial Blessing during the closed time, they should be willing to abide by the prescriptions of the liturgy. Since they ask for the blessing during the closed time it is presumed that their principal concern is to receive the spiritual benefits attached to the Nuptial Blessing, and that they are not primarily interested in lavish display.

In conclusion, the writer is of the opinion that the words *nimia pompa* apply only to what takes place in church. The spouses are to be warned to avoid any form of *excessive* display which would be out of keeping with the penitential spirit of Lent and Advent. More specific regulations in this matter can be laid down by the ordinary when he grants the spouses permission to receive the Nuptial Blessing.

A matter related to the prohibition of the Nuptial Blessing during the forbidden times is the prohibition of the same blessing during the time of a general local interdict,[74] even on the more

[69] *De Matrimonii Celebratione*, n. 70.

[70] *De Matrimonio*, n. 1953, p. 322.

[71] *Ius Matrimoniale*, n. 575.

[72] *De Matrimonio*, n. 710.

[73] "The Meaning of Solemnities,"—*Australsian Catholic Record*, XV (1938), 173.

[74] Can. 2271: "Si interdictum fuerit locale generale et interdicti decreto aluid non caveatur expresse. . . .

2° In ecclesia cathedrali, ecclesiis paroecialibus vel in ecclesia quate

solemn days on which the interdict is suspended.[75] The blessing is also forbidden during a particular local interdict with regard to the church which is under interdict.[76] Those who are under personal interdict are forbidden to receive the blessing in view of the rule expressed in canon 2275.[77]

An interesting point in connection with the question of the forbidden times is the indult enjoyed by the Indians and Negroes of Latin America and of the Philippine Islands. The Constitution

unica sit in oppido, in iisque solis, permittitur . . . assistentia matrimoniis, exclusa benedictione nuptiali. . . ."

[75] Can. 2270, § 2: "In die Nativitatis Domini, Paschatis, Pentecostes, sanctissimi Corporis Christi et Beatae Mariae Virginis in caelum assumptae, interdictum locale suspenditur, et prohibetur tantum collatio ordinum et sollemnis nuptiarum benedictio."

[76] Can. 2272, § 3: "Si latum fuerit [interdictum locale] in certam ecclesiam vel oratorium: . . . 2° Si fuerit paroecialis, servetur praescriptum cit. can. 2271, n. 2, nisi interdicti decretum aliam ecclesiam pro interdicti tempore eidem substituat."

[77] Can. 2275: "Personaliter interdicti. . . . 2° Prohibentur Sacramenta et Sacramentalia ministrare, conficere et recipere, ad normam can. 2260, § 1, 2261."

Can. 2260, § 1: "Nec potest excommunicatus Sacramenta recipere; imo post sententiam declaratoriam aut condemnatoriam nec Sacramentalia.

Can. 2261, § 1: "Prohibetur excommunicatus licite Sacramenta et Sacramnetalia conficere et ministrare. . . . At first sight it would seem that before sentence had been passed a personally interdicted person could lawfully receive the Nuptial Blessing since this is only a sacramental. However it must be remembered that canons 2275 and canons 2260-2261 forbid such a person, even before any sentence has been passed, to administer or receive the sacraments. The Nuptial Blessing is ordinarily received on the occasion of the reception and administration of the Sacrament of Matrimony, of which sacrament the parties are both the recipients and the ministers. Furthermore canon 1066 regarding the marriage of those notoriously under censure should be also borne in mind in this regard. Even supposing the Nuptial Blessing is administered apart from the actual reception of the Sacrament of Matrimony, as provided for in canon 1101, § 1, the incongruity of the situation in which a personally interdicted person would receive the solemn public official blessing of the Church is too apparent to required comment.

Trans Oceanum allows them to receive the Nuptial Blessing at any time of the year without any special permission of the Ordinary.[78]

[78] Leo XIII, litt. ap. "*Trans Oceanum,*" 18 apr. 1897, n. XI—*Fontes,* n. 633.

CHAPTER VII

THE PLACE FOR THE CELEBRATION OF MARRIAGE

Canon 1109

§ 1. Matrimonium inter catholicos celebretur in ecclesia paroeciali; in alia autem ecclesia vel oratorio sive publico sive semi-publico, nonnisi de licentia Ordinarii loci vel parochi celebrari poterit.

§ 2. Matrimonium in aedibus privatis celebrari Ordinarii locorum in extraordinario tantum aliquo casu et accedente semper iusta ac rationabili causa permittere possunt; sed in ecclesiis vel oratoriis sive Seminarii sive religiosarum, Ordinarii id ne permittant, nisi urgente necessitate, ac opportunis al hibitis cautelis.

Canon 1109 treats of the place for the celebration of marriage. In paragraphs one and two the marriages of Catholics are considered; in paragraph three the canon legislates for the place of mixed marriages. This latter paragraph will be treated in Chapter VIII along with paragraph two of canon 1102, which discusses the rites for mixed marriages, and of which mention is made in canon 1109, § 3. These two paragraphs will be discussed under the general heading of "The Celebration of Mixed Marriages."

Paragraph one of canon 1109 gives the general rule for the marriages of Catholics, while paragraph two treats of two exceptions to the general rule. The discussion of canon 1109, § 1, and § 2, will be treated in three articles. First the general rule will be commented upon, then the first exception, namely that of marriages in private houses, will be discussed, and finally the other exception, namely that of marriages in the churches or oratories of seminaries and of women religious, will be treated.

ARTICLE I—THE GENERAL RULE

The general rule for the place of the marriages of Catholics is set forth in paragraph one of canon 1109 as follows: "Marriage between Catholics shall be contracted in the parish church, and cannot take place in another church or oratory, whether public or semi-public, without the permission either of the local ordinary or of the pastor." The explanation of this paragraph will be given under the following headings. A. In general marriage should take place *in church*. B. As a rule in the *parish church*. C. The permission of the pastor or of the local ordinary is required that it may be celebrated *in another church* than the parish church.

A. *Marriage to Be Celebrated in Church*

It will be helpful to compare the former law with the law of the Code on this point.

1.—The Former Law

The general law of the Council of Trent, when it issued the decree *Tametsi* regarding the canonical form of marriage, did not prescribe any special place for the celebration of marriage. However, the Church's wish in the matter seemed to be indicated in the wording of the decree: ". . . let the marriage be celebrated *in facie Ecclesiae ubi parochus, etc.*"[1] The mind of the Church was even more apparent from the wording of the Ritual issued by Paul V on June 17, 1614: "*matrimonium in ecclesia maxime celebrari decet.*"[2] Hence, though marriage could lawfully be celebrated in any decent place, whether sacred or otherwise, it was the wish of the Church that it be performed in the sacred edifice. If there was question of the Nuptial Blessing contained in the Nuptial Mass, this regularly had to be imparted in Church, since it could not, except by special indult, be separated from the Holy Sacrifice.[3]

[1] Sess. XXIV, *de ref. matrim.*, c. 1. also *supra*, pp. 21-23.

[2] *Rituale Romanum*, Tit. VII, *de sacramento matrimonii*, C. I, n. 16.

[3] In this case the actual marriage according to the ceremonies of the Ritual would ordinarily take place in church immediately before the Nuptial Mass. Sometimes however the marriage was contracted at home, and only some days later did the spouses come to the church to receive the Nuptial Blessing. Cf. *Rituale Romanum*, Tit. VII, *de sacramento matrimonii*, C. I, n. 16. Regarding the practice of contracting the actual marriage before the doors of the church cf. *supra*, pp. 37-42.

Therefore it was the wish of the Council of Trent and of the supreme pontiffs that marriage should be celebrated in church. Consequently bishops and provincial councils were within their rights when they forbade the celebration of marriage in private homes and commanded that they be performed in church.[4]

It is not difficult to understand why the Holy See should desire that marriages should be celebrated in church. Marriage is a sacrament, and the church is the proper place for the administration of the sacraments. Furthermore, besides its religious nature, marriage has a social aspect. It is a contract public by nature and fraught with many effects on society. Therefore it should be celebrated publicly, with the offices of the Church, and in the place destined for public worship. In recent times the Congregation of the Sacraments has indicated an added reason for the Church's attitude in this matter. On the occasion of a response forbidding the celebration of a funeral Mass in the home, the observations of the Reverend Consultors regarding the question were also published. Observation number four reads as follows:

> 4. Finally, there is yet another very weighty argument. All are aware that there is a certain tendency and propensity among the faithful to withdraw from sacred places even the most sacred ceremonies of the Church. We all know that, even since the promulgation of the Code, the faithful in many places wish to continue the custom which has arisen through abuse, namely, that of allowing infants to be baptized at home, marriages to be contracted in a room of the house, and other such rites to be performed outside of the church. It is a sort of attempt to laicize—if that word may be permitted—the ceremonies of the Church. Being unable to destroy them, wicked men strive at least to rob them of their accidental sanctity; and the faithful passively acquiesce. The Code has tried vigorously to resist the weakness (cf. cc. 773, 1109, § 1, and § 2) and let us hope with

[4] Pages 44-49 of the historical section of this work furnish many examples of such legislation. The opinion of Barbosa and others, who held that the bishop could not forbid marriage in private houses, is there discussed. Cf. also Wernz-Vidal, *Ius Matrimoniale,* n. 579, note 28.

success. Hence such cases are not to be multiplied, but restricted as far as possible.[5]

2.—The Present Law

Before the Code there was no general law which prescribed that marriages be performed in church, although the ecclesiastical authorities earnestly desired that they take place there. In the present law that which was a counsel in earlier times has become strictly preceptive. For the first time in the general law of the Church there appears a prohibition against the celebration of marriage in private houses, due allowance being made for extraordinary cases. For the first time also there is a command that marriage be celebrated in church, and as a general rule in the parish church.

B. *Marriage to be Celebrated in the Parish Church*

Among the reserved parochial functions which are enumerated by canon 462 is the right to assist at marriages and to impart the Nuptial Blessing.[6] As Payen observes, it is clear that the Code contemplates these functions as being exercised in the pastor's own church.[7] Therefore canon 1109, § 1, is in accord with canon 462, 4°,when it states the general rule that marriages should take place in the parish church. Consequently no one but the ordinary can demand of the pastor that he permit a marriage in a church or oratory other than the parish church.[8]

Ordinarily the parish church of the bride will be the place of celebration, but it is lawful to celebrate the marriage in the parish church of either party. If the bride has several parish churches by reason of domicile, quasi-domicile, or the canonical "month's residence," she is at liberty to choose any one of these parish churches in which to be married.[9]

[5] S.C. de Sacr., *Romana et aliarum*, 3 maii 1926—*AAS*, XVIII (1926), 388. English translation from Bouscaren, *Canon Law Digest*, I, 390.

[6] Can. 462: "Functiones parocho reservatae sunt, nisi aliud iure caveatur: . . . 4° . . . matrimoniis assistere; nuptialem benedictionem impertiri.

[7] *De Matrimonio*, n. 1959.

[8] Chelodi, Ius Matrimoniale, n. 146.

[9] Cf. canon 1097, § 1, and § 2.

C. *Marriage in a Church other than the Parish Church*

That the marriage be celebrated in another church besides the parish church, or in a public or semi-public oratory,[10] excepting the churches or oratories of seminaries and of women religious, no special reason is demanded by the Code, although such a reason will usually be present. All that is required is the permission of the ordinary (the bishop or his vicar-general) in whose diocese th church or oratory is situated, or of the pastor in whose parish such a church or oratory lies. This pastor will assist at the marriage or give delegation to the one who is to perform the marriage, unless the delegation has already been obtained from the ordinary. If the parish in which the marriage is to be performed is not the parish of either of the contracting parties by reason of domicile, quasi-domicile, or "month's residence," there will be required for lawfulness the permission of the pastor of one of the contracting parties, and also a certificate of the freedom of the parties to marry.[11]

Thus the second part of paragraph one constitutes an exception to the general rule that the marriage be performed in the parish church, but, as Payen notes, this exception deals with ordinary cases and is readily permitted.[12] The same cannot be said

[10] It will be helpful to recall here the Code's definition of a church and of the various types of oratories. According to canon 1161 the term "church" signifies a sacred edifice dedicated to divine worship, especially with a view to enabling all the faithful to participate in public worship. Canon 1188 defines an oratory as a place destined for divine worship, but not with the principal object of serving the faithful at large for public worship. An oratory is called: 1° *public,* if it has been erected mainly for the convenience of some associated group, or even of private individuals, but in such a manner that all the faithful have a legitimately established right to enter the oratory, at least at the time of divine services; 2° *semi-public,* if it has been erected for the convenience of some community or of a group of the faithful who meet there, and access to it is not indiscriminately free to everyone; 3° *private* or *domestic,* if it has been erected in a private house for the exclusive benefit of some family or of a private individual.

[11] Cf. canon 1020, 1021, 1096, 1097, 1103.

[12] *De Matrimonio,* n. 1959, p. 327, note 3.

for the exceptions which are to be treated now. The first, namely, the celebration of marriage in private houses, is permitted only in an extraordinary case; the second, i.e., the celebration of marriage in churches or oratories of seminaries and of women religious, is allowed only in a case of necessity.

Article II—The First Exception

The first exception is stated in the first part of paragraph two of canon 1109 as follows: "The local ordinary may not permit the celebration of marriage in private houses except in some extraordinary case and for a good reason." Except under the conditions set forth by the canon, the celebration of marriage in private houses, even in those which have a domestic oratory wherein Mass may be celebrated, is interdicted by the Code. Gasparri believes, however, that in the case of a domestic oratory which has the privilege of the celebration of Mass, a lesser reason would suffice than that required for the celebration of marriage in an ordinary private house. He adds that marriage can be celebrated in the chapel of the episcopal residence, or of any Apostolic Nuncio or Delegate, or of a Cardinal, in virtue of a privilege which the Holy See usually grants to such personages.[13] In any case it is to be noted that such chapels, although private, enjoy all the rights and privileges of semi-public oratories.[14] Therefore they are not included in the restriction of paragraph two of canon 1109, but rather come under paragraph one of the same canon. Hence, even in the case wherein they would not have the special privilege for the celebration of marriage mentioned by Gasparri, if there be such a case, the "extraordinary case" of § 2 would not have to be present in order that the celebration of marriage might be permitted.

It is to be noted that only the local ordinary, i. e., the bishop or his vicar general, or, *sede vacante,* the administrator, can

[13] *De Matrimonio* (ed. nova), n. 1066.

[14] Can. 1189: "Oratoria S. R. E. Cardinalium et Episcoporum sive residentialium sive titularium, licet privata, fruuntur tamen omnibus iuribus et privilegiis quibus oratoria semi-publica gaudent."

grant the dispensation mentioned in paragraph two of canon 1109; hence the pastor is not empowered to grant such permission.

Before the dispensation may be granted two conditions must be verified. The case must be an extraordinary one, one which is not of frequent occurrence. It is clear, then, that the bishop could not give a general dispensation to a certain group or to a certain family.[15] The second condition is that there must be a just and reasonable cause, in other words, a cause proportionate to the concession granted. Hence a very urgent cause, e. g., serious illness of one of the parties, is not required. Examples of a sufficient cause are: the necessity of secretly convalidating a marriage which is invalid for some reason not known to the general public; great difficulty in getting to the church, as is frequently the case in missionary dioceses;[16] ridicule or some other notable inconvenience which is feared because of the number of people who would be present were the marriage to be celebrated in church.[17] Augustine lists as a sufficient cause the case of a benefactor either of the parish or of the diocese, who has a private chapel in his home.[18] And Vermeersch-Creusen say that this permission may quite readily be granted to Catholic rulers.[19]

Whether the prohibition of paragraph two of this canon against the celebration of marriages in private houses is to be extended also to mixed marriages, which are forbidden to be celebrated in church by paragraph three of the same canon, will be discussed in the following chapter, which treats of the celebration of mixed marriages. Suffice it to say here that the prohibition applies also to mixed marriages. Otherwise a consideration would be granted to mixed marriages which Catholic marriages do not enjoy.[20]

Relative to private houses which have a domestic oratory, there may, or there may not exist an indult from the Holy See permitting the celebration of Mass. In the first case the permission to

[15] Payen, *De Matrimonio,* n. 1959-bis.

[16] Payen, *De Matrimonio, loc. cit.*

[17] Vlaming, *Praelectiones,* n. 616.

[18] *Marriage Law,* p. 322.

[19] *Epitome,* II, n. 413.

[20] Cf. Vermeersch-Crusen, *Epitome,* II, n. 413.

celebrate the marriage carries along with it the permission to celebrate the Nuptial Mass and impart the Nuptial Blessing in accordance with the rubrics. In the latter case the ordinary can permit the celebration of Mass *per modum actus* [21] and hence also the imparting of the Nuptial Blessing.

As Payen notes, the canon contemplates places where the Church is well organized, and where there is an ample number of churches. In missionary countries and dioceses, if in a certain territory there is no church or oratory, either public or semi-public, the missionary does not need any special permission to celebrate marriage in private homes. The principle *ad impossible nemo tenetur* applies there. Further, if by virtue of his faculties the missionary is permitted to say Mass in private homes, there is nothing to prevent him from saying the Nuptial Mass and from imparting the solemn Nuptial Blessing in private houses.[22]

It goes without saying that if marriage is to be celebrated outside of church, it must be celebrated in a decent place. Cappello mentions a private chapel and the parish house as suitable places.[23]

Article III—The Second Exception

The latter part of paragraph two of canon 1109 gives the second exception to the general rule: "The ordinary shall not permit marriages to take place in the churches or chapels of seminaries or of women religious, except in a case of urgent necessity, and with due precautions."

Since urgent necessity is required for the ordinary to dispense from this prescription of the law, the projected case will be of rare occurrence. An example of urgent necessity would be had in a locality wherein there was no other oratory or church.

Payen, in solving a case on the point in question, says that the urgent necessity demanded by paragraph two can be verified not only by a physical need, as in the case wherein no other church or chapel is available, but also by a moral exigency. This moral

[21] Cf. canon 1195, § 2.

[22] Payen, *De Matrimonio,* n. 1959-bis.

[23] *De Matrimonio,* n. 728.

exigency can, from the viewpoint of practical considerations, set up so serious a need that it becomes the equivalent of an urgent necessity. In the case he discusses Payen contemplates the situation in which the house of the women religious has drawn, with profit to the mission as well as to themselves, upon the benevolent generosity of the families of the spouses. He considers the granted permission for the celebration of the marriage in the sisters' chapel as an act of refined courtesy and urbanity, the need of which in the special circumstances measures up to the urgent necessity which canon 1109 requires. He adds further that when there is question of the chapel of women religious who devote their energies to the education of young women, and who are bound simply by the episcopal cloister, the ruling with regard to the urgent necessity may be interpreted quite reasonably with a fair degree of liberality. And, finally, Payen adverts to the additional fact that in such a supposition there would be comparatively less need of stringent precautions, inasmuch as eventual detrimental consequences would be considerably minimized.[24]

It is evidently the purpose of the latter part of paragraph two of canon 1109 to insure the proper moral safeguards for the vocatious seminarians and the women religious. The place where souls are being trained to a celibate life should not suffer the encroachment of marriage solemnities, even though they be of a religious nature.[25] Hence before the ordinary may permit the celebration of marriage in such a place, the Code requires, besides urgent necessity, the taking of due precautions with a view to averting from the seminarians and from the women religious every possible harm. Such harm could eventuate through the necessitated disruption of important community exercises or through its implied intrusion upon the mental recollection requisite for the cultivation of the true religious and clerical spirit. But when an urgent necessity justifies the granting of permission for

[24] *De Matrimonio*, nn. 1963-1964, *Casus*, 282.

[25] C. D., "De Sacramento Matrimonii,"—*Perfice Munus*, VIII (1933), 901-905, especially p. 905. The danger to vocation would be still greater if the person desiring to be married in a seminary or convent chapel were an ex-seminarian or an ex-religious.

the celebration of marriage in seminary or convent chapels, then effective safeguards can normally be invoked by means of the practical requirement on the part of the ordinary that the seminarians or religious be left uninformed about the prospective ceremony, or if this lie outside the range of possibility, that they be held to an order of the day that will ensure their absence from the chapel at the time of the celebration of the marriage.[26]

In consideration of the subject matter and purpose of the law, the term, "women religious," is to be interpreted in a broad sense according to Cappello.[27] Hence he extends the prohibition of canon 1109, § 2, also to the chapels of women who live in community life without being subject to public religious vows. In this matter, however, Payen holds a different opinion.[28] It seems that Cappello's opinion is more in accord with the purpose of the law. Both Cappello and Payen, however, agree that the local ordinary can extend the prohibition relative to the celebration of marriage so that it will affect not only any and every religious house properly so called but also any habitation in which either men or women profess the works of religion in common without being bound by religious vows.

[26] Payen, *De Matrimonio,* n. 1959-ter.

[27] *De Matrimonio,* n. 728; cf. also Gasparri, *De Matrimonio* (ed. 1932), n. 1065.

[28] "Ad pias domos mulierum quae non sint religiosae, jus commune non spectat."—*De Matrimonio,* n. 1959-ter.

CHAPTER VIII

THE CELEBRATION OF MIXED MARRIAGES

The preceding chapter treated of the place for the celebration of marriage, and was in effect a commentary on canon 1109 of the Code. It was noted, however, that paragraph three of that canon, which legislates for the place of mixed marriages, would be considered in a separate chapter. The treatment here of the aforementioned paragraph necessarily entails a discussion of canon 1102, § 2, also. The latter considers the liturgical form (more properly the absence of any liturgical form) in mixed marriages, and is referred to in canon 1109, § 3. In the treatment of canon 1102, § 2, it will be useful to consider also, at least briefly, paragraph one of the same canon. That paragraph considers the juridical form for mixed marriages.

It is to be noted that in this chapter the word "mixed marriage" is used in a broad sense, and comprehends not only those marriages which are forbidden by canon 1060, namely, marriages between a Catholic and a heretic or schismatic, but also those marriages which are prohibited by canon 1070, namely, marriages between a Catholic and a non-baptized person. The term "mixed marriage" has been used in this general sense by the Holy See.[1]

Furthermore, it is clear from the wording of the Code that the prescriptions of canon 1109, § 3, which forbids the celebration of mixed marriages in church, and of canon 1102, § 2, which interdicts all sacred rites in the celebration of mixed marriages, apply with equal force to mixed marriages in the strict sense, and to disparate marriages.[2] For canon 1102 and canon 1109, § 3, both use the term *matrimonia inter partem catholicam et partem acatholicam.* Canon 1064, 4°, says that the celebration of mixed marriages in the strict sense is to be governed by canon 1102.

[1] S.C.S. Off. decr. 14 ian. 1932: "Contingit aliquando mixta, quae vocant, matrimonia inter catholicum et acatholicum sive baptizatum sive non baptizatum contrahi. . . . "—*AAS,* XXIV (1932), 25.

[2] Cf. Schenk, *Mixed Religion and Disparity of Cult, nn.* 24-27, for a discussion of the terminology in the matter of "mixed" marriages.

Further, canon 1071 states that all the prescriptions of canons 1060-1064, regarding mixed marriages in the strict sense, are to be applied also to disparate marriages. Hence the celebration of disparate marriages is regulated by canon 1064, 4°, and therefore by canon 1102.

Article I—The Juridical Form in Mixed Marriages

Canon 1102

§ 1. In matrimoniis inter partem catholicam et partem acatholicam interrogationes de consensu fieri debent secundum praescriptum can. 1095, § 1, n. 3.

Canon 1102, § 1,since it requires that in mixed marriages the parties be interrogated concerning their consent in accordance with the prescription of canon 1095, § 1, n. 3,[3] abolishes entirely that "mere passive assistance" which satisfied the requirements of the Tridentine form for validity, and which the Holy See sometimes resorted to in the case of those mixed marriages to which she was unwilling to grant active assistance. When the pastor or his delegate assisted passively at such marriages, he was merely present when the parties exchanged their consent before him; he did not interrogate the parties regarding their consent, nor did he wear any sacred vestment or use any sacred ceremony at the marriage. His role was merely that of an authorized witness whose duty it was to see the marriage performed and to note the fact in the matrimonial register. As is evident, such passive assistance was rendered outside of church.[4]

The decree *Ne temere* required the pastor to question the spouses regarding their consent, and demanded this as a con-

[3] § 1. "Parochus et loci Ordinarius valide matrimonio assistunt: . . . 3° Dummodo neque vi neque metu gravi constricti requirant excipiantque contrahentium consensum."

[4] A very complete history of the growth of the institute of passive assistance and of its final abolition by the Code has been written by Oesterle in his article "Circa Declarationem Authenticam Can. 1102 De Passiva Assistentia," in the *Jus Pontificium,* X (1930), 110-119 and 292-314. Cf. esp. pp. 112-115, "notio assistentiae passivae," and pp. 116-119, "ratio juridica concessionis assistentiae passivae."

dition for the validity of the marriage.[5] Thus passive assistance in the strictest sense of the word was abolished by law.[6] But since the new legislation occasioned some difficulties, the Holy Office on June 21, 1912, declared that purely passive assistance was to be rendered in mixed marriages which were contracted when the usual guarantees had not been given.[7] The same Congregation declared in 1916 that the response of 1912 applied under the same conditions only to those regions in which, before the time of the *Ne temere* decree, the Holy See had granted the use of a purely passive assistance in the case of illicit mixed marriages. Mixed marriages in any other region, when they were contracted without the interrogations on the part of the pastor regarding consent, were declared invalid.[8] Following this response the Holy Office declared that in a case of convalidation, when the non-Catholic party was willing to go before the priest but refused absolutely to give the required guarantees, the case was to be handled by a *sanatio in radice,* and not by a renewal of consent before the pastor assisting merely passively.[9]

With the Code in force on May 19, 1918, passive assistance strictly so called was abolished everywhere. A response of the Holy Office on November 26, 1919, made this clear. Since this decree was not published in the *Acta Apostolicae Sedis* its existence was not known by many, and some authors held that passive assistance was still possible.[10] A reply of the Code Commis-

[5] S.C.C., decr. "*Ne temere,*" 2 aug. 1907—*Fontes,* n. 4340.

[6] S.C.C., *Romana et aliarum,* 27 iul. 1908, ad III: "An vi decreti Ne temere, etiam ad matrimonia mixta valide contrahenda, ab Ordinario vel a parocho exquirendus et excipiendus sit contrahentium consensus." Resp. "Affirm. servatis ad liceitatem quoad reliqua praescriptionibus et instructionibus S. Sedis."—*Fontes,* n. 4350.

[7] *AAS,* IV (1912), 443; cf. Oesterle, *art. cit.,* p. 312.

[8] S.C.S. Off., 3 aug. (approbatum 5 aug., publicatum 1 sept.) 1916—*AAS,* VIII (1916), 316. Cf. also Oesterle, *art. cit.,* p. 313 and notes 2 and 4.

[9] S.C.S. Off., 20 nov. 1916 (approb. 21 nov., datum 22 nov., public. 10 ian. 1917),—*AAS,* IX (1917), 13. Cf. also Oesterle, *art. cit.,* p. 313, note 4.

[10] Wernz-Vidal, *Ius Matrimoniale,* p. 661, note 41: "Quod responsum, cum in A.A.S. non fuerit publicatum passim ignorabatur." The decree

sion in 1928 removed all doubt in the matter. It was asked whether canon 1102, § 1, revokes the faculty which was granted in some places by the Holy See, namely, of assisting passively at illicit mixed marriages. The reply was in the affirmative.[11] The provision which had previously been made was of the nature of a particular law to which the Code law stood opposed. The earlier enactment was not of the nature of a privilege. Hence the ruling of canon 6, 1°, applied in this matter, and not that of canon 4.[12]

Since the Code, therefore, mere passive assistance is abolished. No longer is it possible to assist in any manner at an illicit mixed marriage, namely, at one entered into without a dispensation or without the usual guarantees. A dispensation must be obtained, the guarantees must be given, the pastor must ask and receive the consent of the parties.[13]

De Smet held that it was not improbable that in an urgent case and when there was not enough time to approach the Holy See, the bishop could permit passive assistance by virtue of the power granted him by canon 81.[14] As Schenk notes, the reply of the Code Commission of 1928 indicates that the Church is unwilling that mere passive assistance should again be permitted.[15] Since, therefore, one of the conditions required by canon 81, namely,

was published in the *Linzer Quartalschrift,* LXXIV (1921), 249. It is found in full in De Smet, *De Spons. et Mat.,* p. 448, note 1. In effect it says that after the advent of the Code a priest cannot assist at mixed marriages unless the promises have been given and a dispensation from the impediment of mixed religion or of disparity of worship has been obtained. The matrimonial consent of the parties must be asked for and received according to the norms of canons 1102 and 1095.

[11] *PCI,* 10 mar. 1928—*AAS,* XX (1928), 120.

[12] Cappello, *De Matrimonio,* n. 715; Cicognani, *Canon Law* (2. ed., auth. English trans. by O'Hara-Brennan, The Dolphin Press: Philadelphia, 1935), p. 479; Oesterle, *art. cit.,* p. 314.

[13] Cf. canons 1060-1064, esp. 1064, 4°; also canons 1095, § 1, 3°, and 1102, § 1. Canon 1071 calls for the application of the same discipline in all cases of disparate marriages.

[14] *De Spons. et Mat.,* p. 448, note 4. This work of De Smet appeared in 1927. The Code Commission gave its reply in 1928.

[15] *Mixed Religion and Disparity of Cult,* n. 386. Cf. also Aertnys-Damen, *Theologia Moralis,* II, n. 706.

that the dispensation in question be one which the Holy See usually grants, is lacking, De Smet's opinion is no longer tenable.

ARTICLE II—THE LITURGICAL FORM IN MIXED MARRIAGES

Canon 1109

§ 3. Matrimonia vero inter partem catholicam et partem acatholicam extra ecclesiam celebrentur; quod si Ordinarius prudenter iudicet id servari non posse quin graviora oriantur mala, prudenti eius arbitrio committitur hac super re dispensare, firmo tamen praescripto can. 1102, § 2.

Canon 1102

§ 2. Sed in matrimoniis inter partem catholicam et partem acatholicam omnes sacri ritus prohibentur; quod si ex hac prohibitione graviora mala praevideantur, Ordinarius potest aliquam ex consuetis ecclesiasticis caeremoniis, exclusa semper Missae celebratione, permittere.

Because of the intimate connection between them, canons 1109, § 3, and 1102, § 2, are treated together under the general heading of "The Liturgical Form in Mixed Marriages." Both taken together repeat in its entirety the former law on the matter of the place and of the rites of mixed marriages. As outlined in the historical section, it has been the practice of the Holy See, ever since it began to grant dispensations for mixed marriages, to forbid the use of any sacred rite at these marriages.[16] And at least from the beginning of the nineteenth century it has been the rule for these marriages to be celebrated outside of church.[17] These rules applied equally to properly permitted as well as to illicitly contracted mixed marriages, i. e., to those which were contracted without a dispensation or without the usual guarantees in those countries where in order to avoid greater evils for

[16] *Schenk, Mixed Religion and Disparity of Cult,* n. 107, note 60.
[17] Schenk, *op. cit.,* pp. 279-280, and note 89.

the Church at the hands of the civil authorities, the Holy See very reluctantly permitted the priest to assist merely passively at such marriages. If the mixed marriage could be contracted in full accordance with the law of the Church upon the previously granted dispensation, then the popes permitted some of the usual ceremonies attaching to a Catholic marriage to be employed whenever the denial of such ceremonies would in all probability have become the occasion of even greater evils.

When dispensations were granted for mixed marriages these general rules were sometimes explicitly stated in the rescript, at other times they were not, although they were always implicitly understood. This variance of procedure caused differences in the practice of assisting at such marriages. To restate the law of the Church in the matter of such dispensations, Pope Pius IX, through his Secretary of State, Cardinal Antonelli, issued in 1858 the Instruction *Etsi Sanctissimus* (sometimes referred to as the *Instructio Antonelliana*), which was to be the unvarying norm in this matter in the future.[18] After stating that the Holy See permits mixed marriages for grave reasons only, and after the usual *cautiones* have been given, the Instruction proceeds:

> Iam vero quod attinet ad praedictas conditiones, de his nempe mixtis nuptiis extra Ecclesiam, et sine parochi benedictione, alioque sacro ritu celebrandis . . . Sanctissimus Dominus noster . . . iussit in posterum, unam eamdemque formulam esse adhibendam ab omnibus Congregationibus. Itaque . . . D.N. constituit, in harum dispensationum concessione utendam esse formulam illius rescripti, quo etiamsi conditiones praedictae de mixtis hisce coniugiis extra Ecclesiam, et absque parochi benedictione, alioque ecclesiastico ritu celebrandis haud aperte declarantur, tamen implicite continentur. Ac Sanctitas Sua omnes Archiepiscopos, Episcopos, aliosque locorum Ordinarios vehementer in Domino monet, hortatur, et excitat, eisque mandat, ut cum ipsi in posterum huius rescripti formula ab hac Sancta Sede obtinuerit facultatem dispensandi super impedimento mixtae religionis, in eadem facultate exsequenda nunquam desistant omni cura, studioque advigilare, ut sedulo quoque impleantur conditiones de mixtis hisce matrimoniis extra Ecclesiam, et absque parochi benedictione, alioque eccle-

siastico ritu celebrandis. Quodsi in aliquibus locis sacrorum Antistites cognoverint easdem conditiones impleri haud posse, quin graviora exinde oriantur damna ac mala, in hoc casu tantum Sanctitas Sua ad huiusmodi maiora damna ac mala vitanda, prudenti eorundem sacrorum Antistitum arbitrio committit, ut ipsi, salvis firmisque semper, ac perdiligenter servatis cautionibus . . . iudicent quando commemoratae conditiones de contrahendis mixtis hisce nuptiis extra Ecclesiam, et absque parochi benedictione impleri minime possint, et quando in promiscuis hisce coniugibus ineundis tolerari queat mos adhibendi ritum pro matrimoniis contrahendis in dioecesano Rituali legitime praescriptum, exclusa tamen semper Missae celebratione, ac diligentissime perpensis omnibus rerum, locorum, ac personarum adiunctis, etque onerata ipsorum Antistitum conscientia super omnium circumstantiarum veritate, et gravitate. Summopere autem exoptat Sanctitas Sua ut iidem sacrorum Antistites huiusmodi indulgentiam, seu potius tolerantiam eorum arbitrio et conscientiae omnio commissam, maiori, quo fieri potest, silentio ac secreto servent.

It is evident from the above text that the Code restates in summary fashion the former law.[19] A reply of the Holy Office in 1862 explained the meaning of the words *ad vitanda graviora mala et damna* used in the above Instruction.[20] This part, as well as that part of the same decree which explains the words of the *Instructio Antonelliana* which enjoin secrecy on the bishops in regard to the concession of sacred rites, will be explained fully later. An encyclical letter of the Congregation of the Propagation of the Faith in 1868 complains that the *Etsi Sanctissimus* had been incorrectly understood by some as a mitigation of the Church's severe attitude towards mixed marriages, and urges bishops to promulgate to priests and people the true doctrine of

[18] Secret, Status, instr. 15 nov. 1858, iussu Pii PP IX—*Fontes,* n. 6454.

[19] Vlaming, *Praelectiones,* I, n. 225, c.: "Ita can. 1102, § 2, qui his verbis summo capite refert Instructionem die 15 nov. 1858 iussu Pii IX a Secretario Status Card. Antonelli ad omnes episcopos directam."

[20] S.C.S. Off. litt. (ad Vic. Ap. Myssurien.), 26 nov. 1862—*Fontes,* n. 971

the Church concerning mixed marriages. In order that a dispensation may be granted for such marriages it does not suffice to obtain the usual guarantees; over and above these there must exist grave reasons for granting the dispensation. If the *Instructio Antonelliana* in some cases permits sacred rites to be employed at such marriages, it tolerates them only by way of exception.[21]

The above documents contain laws which are identical with those which are found in the Code, and therefore the present laws must be interpreted in the light of these documents and from viewpoint of the explanation given of them by approved authors before the Code.[22]

In the treatment of canons 1102, § 2, and 1109, § 3, the following order will be followed. A. The general rule concerning the omission of the liturgical form. B. The reasons for this rule. C. The exceptions to the general rule.

A—*The General Rule*

In the previous article it was seen that purely passive assistance at mixed marriages was abolished by the Code. No longer can the priest permit the parties merely to exchange their consent in his presence, since canon 1102, § 1, requires that he interrogate them regarding their consent, in accordance with the prescription of canon 1095, § 1, 3°. However the assistance required by canon 1102, may in a certain sense be called a passive

[21] S.C. de Prop. Fide, litt. encycl., 11 mart. 1868: "Quod si aliquando in memorata instructione mos adhibendi ritum pro matrimoniis contrahendis in diocesano Rituali legitime praescriptum, exclusa tamen semper Missae celebratione, in mixtis coniugiis contrahendis tolerari posse perhibetur, id tamen nonnisi per modum exceptionis indulgetur, ac sub conditione ut omnia rerum locorum ac personarum adiuncta diligentissime perpendantur atque onerata Episcoporum conscientia super omnium circumstantiarum veritate ac gravitate. Tantum abest ut inibi principiis, quae Sedes Apostolica circa mixta coniugia quovis tempore professa est, vel minime detrahetur."—*Fontes,* n. 4872.

[22] Can. 6, 2°: "Canones qui ius vetus ex integro referunt, ex veteris iuris auctoritate, atque ideo ex receptis apud probatos auctores interpretationibus, sunt aestimandi."

assistance,[23] since, in accordance with the general rule of § 2 of this canon, the priest does nothing to show his or the Church's approval of mixed marriages. As will be seen later, this was one of the purposes intended by the Holy See when it denied to mixed marriages the accompaniment of any religious ceremony. Briefly, then, according to the strict rule of canons 1102, § 2, and 1109, § 3, the assisting priest is merely to interrogate the parties concerning their consent, and he is to assist outside of church, and to abstain from using any sacred rite. It will be useful to consider in detail which various rites are forbidden, and then to treat of certain rites which are not forbidden, either because they are not strictly *sacred* rites, or because, if they be sacred rites, they do not form part of the marriage ceremony or constitute a complement thereto. Finally, the question of the local factor in connection with the celebration of mixed marriages will be treated separately, as is done in the Code itself.[24]

1—All Sacred Rites are Forbidden

It is clear from the words of canon 1102, § 2, *"exclusa semper Missae celebratione,"* that the Nuptial Mass is forbidden, as is also on the days on which the Nuptial Mass is not permitted, the Mass of the day with a commemoration of the Nuptial Mass.

[23] Cf. Oesterle, "Circa Declarationem Authenticam Can. 1102 de Passiva Assistentia,"—*Jus Pontificium,* X (1930), esp. p. 115, notes 2 and 3, regarding the different meanings of the term "passive assistance."

[24] Pre-Code law in general considered the factors touching the rites and the place of celebration simultaneously. The phrase adopted by the *Instructio Antonelliana,* "extra ecclesiam, et absque parochi benedictione ulloque alio ecclesiastico ritu," is found substantially the same in many responses of the Sacred Congregations. Cf. S.C.S. Off. (Quebec), 10 sept. 1820—*Fontes,* n. 859; instr. (ad Archiep. Quebecen.), 16 sept. 1824, ad 5—*Fontes,* n. 866; (Vic. Ap. Sandwic.), 11 dec. 1850, ad 22, 24—*Fontes,* n. 913; instr. (ad Archiep. Corcyren.), 3 ian. 1871, n. 3—*Fontes,* n. 1013; S.C. de Prop. Fide, instr. (ad Vic. Ap. Sveciae), 6 sept. 1785—*Fontes,* n. 4606; instr. (ad Ep. Graeco-Rumen.), a. 1858—*Fontes,* n. 4843; Secret. Status, instr. (Card. Albani), 27 mar. 1830—*Fontes,* n. 6451.

From a response of the Holy Office in 1872,[25] and from a reply of the Code Commission in 1925 it is evident that not only is the Nuptial Mass prohibited (and hence also the Mass of the day in which the Nuptial Mass is commemorated), but any Mass which from the attendant circumstances could be considered as a complement to the marriage ceremony. The Code Commission was asked: "Whether c. 1102, § 2, besides prohibiting the Mass *pro sponsis* in mixed marriages, prohibits also another Mass, though it be a private one." The reply was: "In the affirmative, if this Mass may from the circumstances be regarded as a complement to the marriage ceremony." [26]

Since the Nuptial Mass or its commemoration is forbidden, therefore the Nuptial Blessing, which is given when the Nuptial Mass is said or commemorated, is likewise prohibited. The special form of the Nuptial Blessing which is found in the appendix to the new Ritual, and which is to be imparted outside of Mass by special indult when the Nuptial Blessing is permitted, but for one reason or another the Mass is not said,[27] seems equally to be forbidden. Although differing from the Nuptial Blessing imparted during Mass, nevertheless it is entitled *benedictio nuptialis* in the Ritual, in contradistinction to formula II in the appendix which is headed *preces recitandae*. Furthermore the *benedictio nuptialis* under n. I cannot be imparted even to Catholics during the forbidden times, or in the case in which the bride is a widow who

[25] SC.S. Off., 17 ian. 1872, ad I: "Utrum vigore clausulae "exclusa semper Missae celebratione" quae apponitur in rescriptis de matrimoniis mixtis prohibeatur tantum Missa *pro sponsis* cum orationibus et benedictionibus uti in Missali Romano, an quaelibet Missa etiam privata quae celebretur coram sponsis et comitibus, post matrimonium, licet sponsis non detur distincta sedes." Resp. "Affirm. respondendum esse ad utramque partem quando Missa celebretur cum omnibus expositis circumstantiis, ita ut habeatur tamquam complementum caermoniae matrimonii."—*Fontes*, n. 1020.

[26] *PCI*, 10 nov. 1925—*AAS* XVII (1925), 583. English translation in Bouscaren, *Canon Law Digest*, I, 546. The case in which the mass would not appear as a complement to the marriage ceremony will be seen below under n. 2.

[27] *Rituale Romanum* (ad normam Codicis), Appendix, De Matrimonio, I; cf. *supra* p. 79.

has received the Nuptial Blessing at her first marriage. These very restrictions indicate that this blessing is a true Nuptial Blessing, an official public blessing of the Church; it consequently seems contrary to the spirit at least of canon 1102, § 2, to permit this blessing at a mixed marriage, even when, in order to avoid greater evils, some of the customary Ritual ceremonies are permitted. In fact, the canon says *aliquam ex* consuetis *caeremoniis,* and this special Nuptial Blessing which is given outside of Mass is certainly not one of the *customary* ceremonies, since a special indult is required in order that it may be imparted.[28]

The imparting of the simple blessing of the Roman Ritual contained in the words, *"Ego coniungo vos in matrimonium. In nomine Patris, et Filii, + et Spiritus Sancti. Amen,"* is likewise interdicted in mixed marriages.[29] As Augustine notes, after the

[28] Schenk and Cerato seem to be the only authors who have adverted to this special Nuptial Blessing in this connection. Schenk says unequivocally that it is prohibited in mixed marriages. Cf. *Mixed Religion and Disparity of Cult,* p. 274, note 67. Cerato thinks that the ordinary could approach the Sacred Congregation of Rites for an indult to permit the special Nuptial Blessing of n. I, or the prayers under n. II of the appendix, *si secus graviora mala praevideantur.* He reasons that the celebration of Mass alone is absolutely forbidden in mixed marriages. Further, while admitting the formula under n. I is a true Nuptial Blessing, he says that if the ordinary cannot be reached, then the parish priest, even without apostolic indult, could permit this blessing or the prayers of n. II to avoid the possible greater evils which would be occasioned by its refusal. He also declares that the ordinary can permit the same *formulae* if recourse to the Holy See is difficult, and the use of these *formulae* is necesary to avoid greater evils. Cf. Cerato, *Matrimonium A Codice I. C. Integre Desumptum* (4. ed. concordatis pro Italia legibus aucta et iuxta illas concinnata, atavii: Libr. Gregoriana edidit typis Seminarii, 1929), pp. 169-171. It is difficult to see how either of these *formulae* would be necessary to avoid greater evils. All the authors place as the limit of the Church's indulgence in this matter the complete marriage ceremony for Catholic marriages found in the body of the Roman Ritual.

[29] S.C.S. Off., 26 nov. 1835: "Se nei matrimonii misti il sacerdote debba anche astenersi dal pronunziare le parole: Ego vos coniungo in matrionium." Resp. "Parochus assistens matrimoniis mixtis se abstineat."—*Fontes,* n. 873. The giving of this blessing is also barred by the *Instructio Antonelliana,* when it uses the words *absque parochi benedictione,* since it

parties of a mixed marriage have given their consent, and joining hands have said the words, "I, N. N. take thee, etc.", the priest may say, "By the authority committed to me I pronounce you united in the bonds of matrimony." [30]

The blessing of the ring as found in the Roman Ritual is forbidden likewise, as also are the prayers and versicles which follow it.[31]

The use of any liturgical vestments, e. g., the surplice and stole, is likewise interdicted in mixed marriages.[32] As Blat notes, a

is clear that the solemn Nuptial Blessing is not meant. That the words of the simple blessing really contain a blessing has been shown above. cf. pp. 11-12, note 37.

[30] Augustine, *Marriage Law,* p. 309. For the manner of assisting at mixed marriages in the United States cf. also Tanquerey, *Synopsis Theologiae Moralis et Pastoralis* (3 vols., Vol. I [*De Poenitentia, De Matrimonio et Ordine*], 12. ed., 3. post cod., Parisiis, Tornaci (Belg.), Romae: Desclée et Socii, 1936), I, n. 957, note 7. See also O'Kane-Fallon, *Notes on the Rubrics of the Roman Ritual,* n. 999; and the *Priest's New Ritual,* p. 222.

[31] S.C.S. Off., 1 aug. 1821: "Quo ritu assistet sacerdos matrimoniis in quibus pars una est acatholica? Licetne proferre formam, dicere preces, benedicere annulum sponsae haereticae." Resp. "Negative."—*Fontes,* n. 863; S.C.S. Off., 17 ian. 1877, ad 3-4—*NRT,* XX (1888), 463-464. The latter response permits the blessing of the ring at the prudent judgment of the bishop, in accordance with the Instruction *Etsi Sanctissimus;* in other words, it permits it only in-so far as it is necessary to avoid greater evils. Vlaming (*Praelectiones,* n. 225 and note 3) permits a private blessing of the ring by the use of the Ritual *benedictio ad omnia,* if the Catholic bride asks for it. Schenk (*Mixed Religion and Disparity of Cult,* p. 274, note 68) cites against Vlaming, Petrovits (*The New Church Law on Matrimony* [Phila., 1919] n. 197) and Tanquerey (*Synopsis Theologiae Moralis et Pastoralis,* I, n. 914), who say that the ordinary's permission must be had to impart the blessing of the ring. But it is evident from a perusal of the texts cited by Schenk that Petrovits and Tanquerey are speaking of the special blessing of the ring as contained in the marriage ceremony of the Ritual, while Vlaming has in mind the *benedictio ad omnia,* which has no necessary connection with the marriage ceremony. Hence the writer can see nothing untenable in Vlaming's opinion.

[32] S.C.S. Off. *(Rosen.),* 16 iul. 1885, ad 2: "Se si può permettere al sacerdote di portare la cotta e la stola nella funzione." Resp. "Detur Instructio *15 novembris 1858.*"—*Fontes,* n. 1094. In other words their use is per-

priest's asking and receiving the consent of the parties when he is vested in surplice and stole constitutes a sacred rite.[33] Therefore a priest is to assist at such marriages in cassock, and prelates in their customary dress, since the normal clerical dress cannot be properly regarded as falling within the category of sacred vestments.[34]

Vlaming says (evidently supposing that the marriage is permitted to be celebrated in church, or at least in a private chapel) that the candles are not to be lighted.[35] Payen says the same.[36] He bases his argument on Cappello who notes that the candles should be lighted at a Catholic marriage, even though the Ritual says nothing in this regard, precisely because, according to the rules of liturgy, they should be lighted whenever a sacred rite is in progress.[37]

The publication of the banns for mixed marriages is forbidden ordinarily; if they are permitted the norm of canon 1026 must be followed.[38]

mitted only to avoid greater evils. For the cited *Instructio Antonelliana* cf. *Fontes,* n. 6454.

[33] *De Sacramentis,* p. 653 "*Sed omnes sacri ritus,* quales proprie sunt interrobationes solum quando ab induto vestibus sacris fierent, v. gr. cum roccheto et stola, *prohibentur.*"

[34] Rossi, *De Matrimonii Celebratione,* n. 99, note 22: "Nec Vestis talaris nec insignia dignitatis, puta vestes praelatitiae et alia huiusmodi, v.g., quae vulgo dicitur "cappa magna" etc., vestes sacrae intelliguntur." Cf. also Gasparri, *De Matrimonio* (ed. 1904), n. 513.

[35] *Praelectiones,* n. 225, p. 199. Cf. also S.C.S. Off., 17 ian. 1877, ad 2—*NRT,* XX (1888), 464.

[36] *De Matrimonio,* n. 1897, note 5.

[37] *De Matrimonio,* n. 705.

[38] "Publicationes ne fiant pro matrimoniis quae contrahuntur cum dispensatione ab impedimento disparitatis cultus aut mixtae religionis, nisi loci Ordinarius pro sua prudentia, remoto scandalo, eas permittere opportunum duxerit, dummodo apostolica dispensatio praecesserit et mentio omittatur religionis partis non catholicae." Cf. De Smet, *De Spons. et Mat.,* p. 447, note 1.

2—Rites Which are Not Forbidden

While the authors generally exclude a formal sermon,[39] a short exhortation is permitted before or after the ceremony.[40]

It has been shown above that the celebration of Holy Mass is forbidden when it could in any way be construed as a complement to the celebration of the mixed marriage. Of course the priest may say a Mass for the intention of the parties, and may even take a stipend for it,[41] but it would be ill advised, to say the least, to celebrate the Mass immediately following the marriage ceremony and while the married couple and their attendants are still in church.[42] Of course no one can prevent the spouses, after the marriage ceremony, from assisting privately at a Mass which is being celebrated, even if it is being celebrated at their request.[43]

In the supposition that permission has been granted for the celebration of the mixed marriage in church, it can scarcely be considered that the playing of organ music during the ceremony would be barred on the score that it constitutes the performance of a sacred rite.[44] The pastor can permit it at his discretion, unless

[39] E.g. Cappello, *De Matrimonio,* n. 716; Schenk, *Mixed Religion and Disparity of Cult,* n. 388, note 73.

[40] S.C.S.Off. , (Rosen.), 16 iul. 1885, ad 3—*Fontes,* n. 1094. Cf. Kenrick, *Theologia Moralis* (2 vols., Mechliniae, 1861), II, n. 163. "Nil autem vetat conjuges sermone gravi de vinculo matrimonii, quod nullo in rerum eventu solvi queat, contra errorem de divortio vigentem, monere, eosque ad veritatis pietatisque studium exercere."

[41] Augustine *(Marriage Law,* p. 310, note 18) says it would be imprudent to announce such a Mass. Nau *(Marriage Laws of the Code,* p. 163) says that if the Mass is published it would be more prudent to publish it as a special intention.

[42] Nau *(loc. cit.)* says "It is not forbidden to celebrate a Mass for the intention of the Catholic party on the day of the marriage, provided the marriage ceremony does not take place before or after the Msas and is not joined to the Mass in such a manner as to cause people to believe that it is part of the eceremony. . . . The Catholic party has a right to invoke God's blessing upon the marriage and may have it offered for the conversion of the non-Catholic party."

[43] Augustine, *loc. cit.*

[44] "Music at Mixed Marriages,"—*Australasian Catholic Record,* III (1926), 348.

of course the ordinary has made contrary regulations in this regard. The singing of sacred music seems to be forbidden, since it seems to constitute a sacred rite.

The blessing of the ring of the Catholic bride is not prohibited provided that it is done outside the actual marriage ceremony itself, and the *benedictio ad omnia* is used, and not the blessing found in the marriage ceremony of the Roman Ritual.[45]

3—The Place of Celebration

Canon 1109, § 3, expressly states that mixed marriages are to be performed outside of church. This is in agreement with the former law, as contained in the *Instructio Antonelliana.*[46] The phrase *extra ecclesiam* is capable of strict interpretation, hence the sacristy is not included in the prohibition.[47] A decision of the Holy Office even admits that a "remote chapel" adjoining the church may be used for the celebration of a mixed marriage, with the knowledge of the bishop.[48]

Feije is of the opinion that it is better to celebrate the mixed marriage not in the sacristy, but in a place that has no connection with the church.[49] De Smet notes a possible inconvenience resulting from the use of the sacristy for such weddings. The bridal party might wish to enter the church with all the solemnity and

[45] Payen, *De Matrimonio,* n. 1897, p. 281 and note 5.

[46] Secret Status, instr. 15 nov. 1858—*Fontes,* n. 6454.

[47] Cappello, *De Matrimonio,* n. 716; Vlaming, *Praelectiones,* n. 225.

[48] S.C.S. Off., 17 ian. 1877: "An tuta conscientia Episcopus Nancien. in sua dioecesi tolerare posset

1° Quod consensus coniugum, salva forma Trident., *in Sacristia* reciperetur?"

2° Quod, in parochiis ubi sacristia apta et conveniens non adest, consensus reciperetur *in alio loco Ecclesiae adiuncto, ut capella remota,* sine cereis accensis, nec quocumque ornatu speciali?

Ad primum et secundum: *Affirmative."—NRT,* XX (1888), 463-464.

[49] *De Imped. et Disp. Mat.,* n. 571: "in alio loco omnio profano sed decenti. . . ."; cf. also Kenrick, *Theologia Moralis,* II, n. 163; "Haud intra templi ambitum, ideoque vix in sacristia. . . ."

pomp of a Catholic wedding, and pass through the church to the sacristy.[50]

It seems to be the custom in this country to celebrate mixed marriages in the rectory. As Nau observes, however, "sometimes no other suitable place than the church is available. The parish house or sacristy of the churches in many smaller parishes may be too small to accommodate the invited guests." [51] There are cases, too, when there is no parish house, and the priest merely has a room adjoining the church.

Regarding the question of the place for the celebration of mixed marriages there arises a discussion concerning their celebration in private homes. If paragraph three of canon 1109 is taken by itself it contains no prohibition against the celebration of mixed marriages in the home. But paragraph two of the same canon forbids house weddings for Catholics, unless the ordinary in an unusual case and for a just cause permits them. It is not conceivable that the legislator abstracted from paragraph two when he framed paragraph three. It is evidently understood that the phrase *extra ecclesiam* does not give the parties of a mixed marriage the right to have their marriage celebrated in the home. If such were the case the whole purpose of paragraph three of canon 1109 would be defeated, for its intent is to show the Church's aversion to mixed marriages by refraining from any act that would seem to approve them, and thus to deter the faithful from entering such marriages. To permit house weddings in the case of mixed marriages would be construed in the eyes of the faithful as a preference shown to such marriages. Therefore the discipline regarding house weddings must be at least as severe in the case of mixed marriages as it is for that of Catholic marriages.[52]

[50] *De Spons. et Mat.*, p. 447, note 3.

[51] *Manual on the Marriage Laws of the Code of Canon Law* (New York, Cinn.: Pustet, 1934), p. 167.

[52] Hilling, "Eherectliche Kontroversen und Probleme," IV, "Sind Haustrauungen bei gemeischten Ehen erlaubt?"—*AKKR*, CV (1925), 111-113. Cf. *Statuta Dioecesis Bellevillensis lata ac promulgata in Synodo Dioecesana Bellevillensi Quinta die 27 dec. 1939 celebrata* (Belleville, Illi-

The latter part of paragraph three of canon 1109 will be treated below, where the dispensation from the general rule concerning the celebration of mixed marriages is discussed.

B—*Reasons for the Prohibitions of Canons 1102, § 2, and 1109, § 3*

The reasons for the prohibition against the celebration of mixed marriages in church with the sacred rites usually employed in Catholic marriages are clearly given in the Instruction *Etsi Sanctissimus*:

> Adiectae quoque fuere conditiones, ut haec mixta coniugia extra Ecclesiam, et absque parochi benedictione ulloque ecclesiastico ritu celebrari debeant. Quae quidem conditiones eo potissimum spectant, ut in catholicorum animis nunquam obliterentur memoria tum canonum, qui istiusmodi mixta matrimonia detestantur, tum constantissimi illius studii quo Sancta Mater Ecclesia nunquam filios suos avertere ac deterrere ab iisdem mixtis coniugiis in eorum et futurae prolis perniciem contrahendis.[53]

The Church wishes to keep ever alive in the minds of her children her severe prohibitions against the contracting of mixed marriages. and thus hopes to deter them from such dangerous unions. To be consistent, then, she cannot permit anything that would seem to be a tacit approval of those marriages which she tolerates most reluctantly. For these reasons she commands that, as a general rule, such marriages are to take place outside of church, and without any religious rite whatsoever. It is only in order to avoid greater evils that she permits such a rule to be relaxed.

nois: Buechler Printing Co., 1940), Stat. 150 : "In matrimoniis mixtis sacerdotes nec ritus nec preces adhibeant, nec stola et superpelliceo utantur. Ista matrimonia sola receptione mutui consensus extra ecclesiam, non in sacristia, sed in domo paroeciali, sunt celebranda; non vero in domo sponsorum sine *specialissima licentia Episcopi*. In missionibus, ubi non est domus paroecialis, sacerdos potest assistere matrimoniis mixtis in domo sponsi vel sponsae sine speciali licentia Ordinarii."

[53] Secret. Status, instr. 15 nov. 1858—*Fontes*, n. 6454.

The legislation of canons 1102, § 2, and 1109, § 3, then, is quite in accord with the law of canon 1060.[54] and canon 1064, 1°.[55]

Because of the serious reasons which underlie the Church's prohibition against the celebration of mixed marriages in church, and against the use of sacred rites in the celebration of such marriages, Payen is of the opinion that a pastor who nevertheless imparts the solemn Nuptial Blessing is guilty of serious sin. He says furthermore that the pastor likewise sins gravely if he performs the mixed marriage in church with all the Ritual ceremonies of Catholic marriages, unless he has obtained the ordinary's permission.[56]

C—*The Exceptions to the General Rule of Canons 1102, § 2, and 1109, § 3.*

After stating the general rule regarding the place of celebration and the omission of sacred rites in the contracting of mixed marriages the Code goes on to say, in canons 1102, § 2, and 1109, § 3, that the ordinary may relax the law in this matter if he foresees that the strict observance of the general rule would be the occasion of greater evils. To what extent he may go in the relaxation of the law will be seen shortly. First, the meaning of the expression *graviora mala* must be made clear.

1—Graviora Mala

The evil which the Church wishes to avoid by the general rule of canons 1102, § 2, and 1109, § 3, which direct that all mixed marriages are to be celebrated outside of church and without any sacred rites consists in the likelihood that the similarity be-

54 "Severissime Ecclesia ubique prohibet ne matrimonium ineatur inter duas personas baptizatas, quarum altera sit catholica, altera vero sectae haereticae seu schismaticae adscripta." The prohibition of this canon applies also to marriages between an unbaptized person and a Catholic, for canon 1071 says that the law contained in canons 1060-1064 is also to be applied to disparate marriages.

55 "Ordinarii aliique animarum pastores: 1° Fideles a mixtis nuptiis, quantum possunt, absterreant."

56 *De Matrimonio,* n. 1897, p. 281 *in fine.*

tween the celebration of Catholic and of mixed marriages would gradually obliterate in the minds of the faithful the Church's aversion to mixed marriages. When the Church permits a relaxation of the general rules of canons 1102, § 2, and 1109, § 3, she does so only with a view to avoiding evils even greater than those which she wishes to obviate through the prohibitions contained in the general rule.[57] The Instruction *Etsi Sanctissimus* used an expression practically identical with that found in the Code:

> Quod si in aliquibus locis sacrorum Antistites cognoverint, easdem conditiones de mixtis coniugiis extra Ecclesiam absque parochi benedictione, alioque ecclesiastico ritu celebrandis impleri haud posse, quin *graviora* exinde *oriantur damna ac mala,* in hoc casu tantum Sanctitas Sua *ad huiusmodi maiora damna ac mala vitanda,* prudenti eorundem sacrorum Antistitum arbitrio committit . . . etc." [58]

In 1862 the Holy Office declared in a very concrete fashion what some of these greater evils were. Such evils are imminent: 1) if the denial of the blessing in mixed marriages would arouse on the part of heretics animosity and hatred against the faithful and against the Church's laws; 2) if the refusal of the blessing by the pastor would cause the spouses, either before or after the Catholic ceremony, to go before a minister, or to forego the Catholic ceremony altogether and to have the marriage celebrated and a blessing imparted in a Protestant church; 3) if it is feared that the refusal of the requested priestly blessing would cause the *cautiones* to be violated, or, what would be still more detestable, would cause the Catholic party to relinquish the true faith and join a Protestant sect.[59]

[57] Fanfani, *De Iure Parochorum,* n. 327, p. 361: "'Graviora mala'—graviora scilicet illis, quae per hanc prohibitionem removere intendit."

[58] Secret. Status, instr. 15 nov. 1858—*Fontes,* n. 6454.

[59] S.C.S. Off., litt. (ad Vic. Ap. Myssurien.), 26 nov. 1862: "Quid intelligendum sit, sciscitaris, per verba quibus in laudata instructione (15 nov. 1858) innititur, et quasi ligatur facultas seu tolerantia benedicendi mixta matrimonia, scilicet ad vitanda graviora mala et damna. Procul dubio graviora inde oriuntur mala et damna—1. quotiescumque ob dene-

It is clear from the word *similia* that the Holy Office did not wish to exclude all other causes for a relaxation of the law except those which it enumerated in its response. It only intended to give some examples of the *graviora mala* to serve as a guide for the ordinary in forming his judgment in a particular case. In doing so it chose examples that were of more frequent occurrence. The ordinary, then, can permit a relaxation of the law in cases analogous to those cited by the Supreme Congregation.[60]

The Holy Office in the same response explained the meaning of the words of the *Etsi Sanctissimus* enjoining secrecy on the bishops regarding the faculty granted to them of permitting a religious celebration of mixed marriages. The Congregation said that these words are not to be understood in the sense that no one is to learn of the bishop's power in this regard; they signify that the bishop is not to use his faculty indiscriminately, but must consider each case separately. He is not to issue public instructions in this matter, so that the religious celebration of mixed marriages would be the general rule. In a word, he is to use his power cautiously and prudently.[61]

gatam matrimoniis mixtis benedictionem facile excitarentur haereticorum querimoniae et odia adversus fideles, legesque catholicas;—2. quotiescumque denegata a parocho catholico benedictione, sponsi ante vel post coram illo celebratum matrimonium ministellum adeant vel etiam in haeterodoxorum templa conveniant ad sacrilegam benedictionem obtinendam parocho catholico omnino posthabito;—3. quotiescumque insuper timendum esset quod recusata ab ipsis petita benedictione, aut non servarentur necessariae cautiones de amovendo a coniuge catholico perversionis periculo, et de universa prole in catholica religione educanda, aut quod detestabilius foret, ne pars catholica ad haereticorum castra in sui et futurae prolis aeternam perniciem transiret. Evidenter. . . . haec et *similia* sunt gravia illa damna ad quae vitanda Summus Pontifex indulgere seu tolerari posse declaravit ut in matrimoniis mixtis nuptialis impertiretur benedictio."—*Fontes,* n. 971. Note that the blessing referred to is not the solemn Nuptial Blessing contained in the Nuptial Mass, but rather the Ritual blessing, since it is clear from the *Instructio Antonelliana* that the celebration of mass is always forbidden at mixed marriages.

[60] Planchard, "Dispense de Disparité de Culte et de Religion Mixte,"—*NRT,* XV (1883), 573-601, esp. p. 586.

[61] S.C.S. Off. litt. (ad Vic. Ap. Myssurien.), 26 nov. 1862: "Sanctitas

A reply of the Congregation for the Propagation of the Faith addressed to the Greek-Rumanian bishops presents an interesting example of the *gravioro mala* visualized by the above mentioned letter of the Holy Office. The Congregation stated that the Holy See wished the Orientals to observe the same regulations regarding the celebration of a mixed marriage contracted by a Uniate and an "Orthodox" person as those prescribed in the Latin Church for a marriage between a Catholic and a heretic, i. e., such a marriage was to take place outside of church and without any religious rite. But since the bishops represented to the Holy See that the faithful of their dioceses attached such importance to the blessing of the priest on their marriage that there was grave reason to fear that they would go to a schismatic priest to obtain it if it were denied them by their own pastor, the Holy Father, through the Sacred Congregation, authorized the bishops to allow the priestly blessing lest in such cases greater evils would be occasioned by the denial. They were to use this power prudently and with discretion.[62]

Another case of interest is that represented by the Archbishop of Corfu, who claimed that the custom had arisen in his archdiocese of blessing mixed marriages in church. The Holy Office reiterated the prescriptions of the *Instructio Antonelliana* regarding the celebration of mixed marirages, and stated that the custom mentioned by the archbishop could be tolerated only if it had taken such root that its eradication would be the cause of greater evils. The celebration of Mass, however, was never to be permitted.[63]

As has been noted the list of "greater evils" given by the Holy Office was not exhaustive; it implied that other evils of a similar

Sua monitos esse voluit Praesules ut non passim et absque delectu matrimoniis mixtis benedictio impertiatur, nec per publicas instructiones, veluti etiam per modum regulae, tali utantur facultate, sed prudenter admodum et caute, ut oblivioni non traduntur saluberrimae Ecclesiae conditiones, quae semper implicite talibus dispensationibus adiunctae intelliguntur."—*Fontes*, n. 971.

[62] S.C. de Prop. Fide, instr. (ad Ep. Graeco-Rumen.), a. 1858—*Fontes*, n. 4843.

[63] S.C.S. Off. instr. (ad Archiep. Corcyren.) 3 ian. 1871, n. 5—*Fontes*, n. 1013.

nature justified a relaxation of the law. Of all the authors the writer has consulted, however, only two do more than restate the *graviora mala* list by the Holy Office. Payen states that if the non-Catholic party really intends to become a convert, but, due to parental opposition, cannot do so till after marriage, a good reason would exist for permitting some of the usual Ritual ceremonies.[64] Certainly, if there was any possibility that the refusal of some religious rites would cause the prospective convert to lose interest in, or possibly even to become antagonistic to the Church, the danger of a "greater evil," such as is required by the canons and by the former law, would be present. Gougnard lists practically the same case, and also the case in which the granting of a relaxation of the law would be a mark of honor rendered to a Catholic family distinguished for its service to the Church.[65] While the latter case is not as clearly a case in which greater evils would ensue if the strict letter of the law were followed, however there is no doubt that the bishop could permit some form of a religious ceremony if in his prudent judgment he foresaw the likely emergence of such greater evils. In the Code, as in the former law, the bishop is the final judge in the matter. The only restriction imposed by the law is that he does not give the permission at random and indiscriminately, nor proclaim it as a rule, but make prudent and cautious use of his power.[66]

2—The Extent of the Dispensation from the Law of Canons 1102, § 2, and 1109, § 3.

From a perusal of the two canons and of the responses under the former law the Church's attitude is clear in the matter. As has been pointed out in n. 1 above, the Church permits a relaxa-

[64] *De Matrimonio,* n 1899: "Exstaret, ad *tutius* preparandum hoc magnum bonum, justa causa aliquam ex consuetis ecclesiasticis caeremoniis permittendi."

[65] *Tractatus de Matrimonio,* p. 366: "Idem permittitur si habetur fundata spes conversionis partis acatholicae, honor tribuendus familiae optime de religione catholica meritae."

[66] S.C.S. Off. litt. (ad Vic. Ap. Myssurien.), 26 nov. 1862—*Fontes,* n. 971.

tion of the general rule only when greater evils would follow from its strict observance. Her disapproval of mixed marriages has in no way lessened. When she permits the celebration of mixed marriages in church, or with the accompaniment of some religious ceremony she does not wish to appear to have become more indulgent in the matter of mixed marriages. Hence, the whole spirit of the law of canons 1102, § 2, and 1109, § 3, when making a relaxation of the general rule possible, is to allow only so much as is considered sufficient to avoid the "greater evils."

Canon 1109, § 3, after forbidding mixed marriages to be celebrated in church, permits the ordinary to dispense from this rule if he foresees that greater evils will follow from its observance. But the canon immediately adds, *"firmo tamen praescripto can.* 1102, § 2." In other words, the marriage may be celebrated in church, but all sacred rites are to be omitted, unless even some of these be necessary to avoid the evils feared. Therefore, if the concession of the celebration of the mariage in church is, in the prudent judgment of the bishop, sufficient to avoid the "greater evils," then this concession alone should be granted. The priest should assist in cassock, without surplice or stole, and should omit all religious ceremonies, such as the blessing of the ring, or the blessing *"Ego coniungo vos, etc."*

If in addition some religious ceremony is judged to be necessary, then the bishop should permit only those ceremonies which in his judgment are necessary in the particular case to avoid the greater evils that are feared if the ceremony were denied.[67] For example, the use of surplice and stole may be sufficient without any other religious rite.[68] In other words, only as much should

[67] Payen, *De Matrimonio,* n. 1899.

[68] S.C.S. Off. instr. (ad Ep. S. Alberti) 9 dec. 1874, n. 18: "Episcopus pro sua prudentia decernat num satis sit sacredotem uti tantum superpelliceo, omissis precibus et reliquis ritibus."—*Fontes,* n. 1036. Cf. *Synodus Dioecesana Fargensis Prima,* p. 72, stat. 369, n. 2: "Si iusta de causa et licentia Ordinarii in ecclesia celebrari permittantur matrimonia mixta celebratio sine pompa fiat, extra sanctuarium, coram sacerdote veste talari, superpelliceo, stola conveniente induto, cereis accensis; musica, si adhibeatur, sit semper sacra."

be permitted as necessity requires. The Code seems to mean this when it permits *aliquam ex consuetis ecclesiasticis caeremoniis.* It states the limit to which the bishop may go in the words *exclusa semper Missae celebratione.* As has been proved, not only is the Nuptial Mass—and consequently also the Nuptial Blessing—forbidden, but also any mass which from the circumstances would appear to be a complement to the marriage ceremony. The limit, then, of the law's indulgence is the complete Ritual ceremony as employed in the marriages of Catholics. As Wernz-Vidal observe, however, those ordinaries act more prudently, who, even in permitting the Ritual ceremonies, preserve some difference between the celebration of a mixed marriage and of a Catholic marriage.[69]

In practice it may be difficult to determine whether the *graviora mala* which must be presupposed for a relaxation of the strict law regarding the celebration of mixed marriages are present in a particular case. Schenk observes that these evils, greater than the ones arising from the danger of appearing to approve such marriages, may be occasioned by the peculiar circumstances of a particular case or in view of the fixed customs of a particular locality.[70] Certainly the "greater evils" would be present if, in a certain locality wherein the Catholic population constitutes a small minority, the refusal of some form of religious ceremony, at least the celebration of the marriage in church, would increase the already existing prejudice against the Catholic Church and her laws. It has been stressed that the bishop is the final judge in the matter. What in some localities would be a cause of scandal to the faithful might in others be regarded by the faithful as an exemplary discipline and as a commendable practice. With the ever necessary obviation of all scandal for Catholics, a procedure or method which in one locality would disaffect the good will of prospective converts, could under other local circumstances stimulate the justified hope of their conversion.

Two quotations from Nau will serve to close this discussion. "By some it is felt that it would be better to make the ceremony

69 *Ius Matrimoniale,* n. 561, note 44.

70 *Mixed Religion and Disparity of Cult,* n. 388, p. 276.

somewhat more religious than is ordinarily done. In our times it is certainly necessary to impress all with the religious nature of marriage. . . . It is a much discussed question whether, perhaps, it would not be better to have a somewhat more distinctly religious ceremony in order to impress the sanctity of the marriage vows on Non-Catholics. On the other hand, too much ceremony might gives the false impression that the Church is no longer hostile to mixed marriages. In our country it is practically impossible to prevent all mixed marriages."[71]

[71] *Manual on the Marriage Laws of the Code,* p. 164, pp. 167-168.

CONCLUSIONS

1. The marriage of the early Christians was simply the marriage of Roman law, and especially of Roman custom, with a prayer of benediction somewhere added.

2. From the third century, and very probably from apostolic times, the priestly blessing, although not required for validity, was the usual accompaniment of marriages between Christians.

3. It is certain that from the sixth century, and possibly earlier, there existed a special *Missa pro sponsis,* similar to the present one of the Roman Missal.

4. Barbosa's opinion which denied the bishop the power to forbid house weddings, and which deterred the Second Provincial Council of St. Louis from making a strict prohibition in this regard, was unsound. This is concluded from the existence of such a prohibition in numerous local councils from the time of the Council of Trent to the end of the nineteenth century.

5. Particular laws prohibiting the simple celebration of marriage during the forbidden times are suppressed by canon 1108, § 1. Customs with a similar prohibitive import are to be treated according to canon 5. In fact, in the light of canon 1041 any such custom in this matter appears to be a *corruptela iuris,* and hence is to be suppressed.

6. It is fully within the bishop's power to prohibit evening weddings, not only in particular cases, but also by general statute.

7. In spite of the opinion of Vlaming and Gasparri, it is most probable, both intrinsically and extrinsically, that particular legislation in forbidding marriages on Sundays or Holy Days would run counter to the general law of canon 1108, § 1.

8. The only one of the ancient *sollemnitates nuptiarum* forbidden in closed times by the Code is the Nuptial Blessing, De Smet's opinion notwithstanding.

9. The urgent necessity demanded by canon 1109, § 2, in order that marriage may be celebrated in the chapels of seminaries and of women religious, may probably be understood not only of a physical necessity, but also of a moral necessity.

10. The special form of Nuptial Blessing to be imparted by apostolic indult outside of Mass as found in the appendix to the Roman Ritual is forbidden equally with the Nuptial Blessing of the Missal in the celebration of mixed marriages.

11. In mixed marriages the ring of the Catholic bride may be blessed before or after the marriage with the Ritual blessing *ad omnia.*

12. The prohibition of house weddings in canon 1109, § 2, applies, at least with equal force, to mixed marriages.

13. Besides the examples of *graviora mala* cited by the Holy Office, those given by Payen (II, n. 1899) and Gougnard (p. 366) seem to justify the permission of some sacred rite at mixed marriages.

14. The greater evils required by canons 1102, § 2, and 1109, § 3, would be present if, in a certain locality wherein the Catholic population constitutes a small minority, the refusal of some form of religious ceremony, at least the celebration of marriage in church, would increase the already existing prejudice against the Catholic Church and its laws.

BIBLIOGRAPHY

Sources

Acta Apostolicae Sedis, Commentarium Officiale, Romae 1909-

Acta et Decreta Conciliorum Recentiorum, Collectio Lacensis. 7 vols., Frisburgi Brisgoviae, 1870-1890.

Bullarum Diplomatum et Privilegiorum Sanctorum Romanorum Pontificum Taurinensis Editio, 24 vols. et Appendix, Augustae Taurinorum, 1857-1872.

Canones et Decreta Concilii Tridentini, editio Neopolitana a Joseph Palella, Neapoli, 1859.

Codex Iuris Canonici Pii X Pontificis Maximi Iussu Digestus Benedicti Papae XV Auctoritate Promulgatus, Romae, Typis Polyglottis Vaticanis, 1917.

Codex Iuris Canonici Fontes Cura Emi. Petri Card. Gasparri Editi, 9 vols., Romae (later Civitate Vaticana), Typis Polyglottis Vaticanis, 1923-1939. (Vols. VII, VIII, et IX ed. cura et studio Emi. Iustiniani Card. Serédi).

Corpus Iuris Canonici, editio Lipsiensis secunda, denuo edidit post Aemilium Ludovicum Richter Aemilius Freidberg, 2 vols., Lipsiae, 1879-1881.

Decreta Authentica Congregationis Sacrorum Rituum ex actis eiusdem collecta eiusque auctoritate promulgata, 7 vols., Romae, 1898-1927.

Decretales D. Gregorii Papae IX, una cum glossis restitutae, Romae, 1582.

Decretum Gratiani Emendatum et Notationibus una cum Glossis Illustratum, Venetis, 1605.

Hardouin, Ioannes, *Acta Conciliorum et Epistolae Decretales et Constitutiones Summorum Pontificum,* 12 vols., Parisiis, 1715.

Hartzheim, Joseph, *Concilia Germaniae,* 11 vols., Coloniae Augustae Agrippinensium, 1759-1790.

Jaffé, P., *Regesta Pontificum Romanorum ab Condita Ecclesia ad* Annum Post Christum MCXCVIII, 2. ed. correctam et auctam asupiciis G. Wattenbach, curaverunt S. Loewenfeld, F. Kaltenbrunner, P. Ewald, 2 vols., Lipsiae, 1885-1888.

Mansi, Ioannes, *Sacrorum Conciliorum Nova et Amplissima Collectio,* 53 vols. in 59, Parisiis, 1901-1927 (partly a reprint).

Missale Romanum ex Decreto Sacrosancti Concilii Tridentini Restitutum—S. Pii V Pontificis Maximi Iussu Editum Aliorumque Pontificum Sura Recognitum—Pii Papae X Auctoritate Reformatum, et SSmi. D.N. Benedicti XV Auctoritate Vulgatum, Romae, Tornaci, Parisiis: Desclée et Socii, 1933.

Monumenta Germaniae Historica, Legum Sectio I, Capitularia Spuria, Tom. II, ed. Pertz, Hanoverae, reprinted in 1925.

Monumenta Germaniae Historica, Legum Sectio II, Capitularia Regum Francorum, Tom. I, ed. Alfredus Boretius, Hanoverae, 1883.

Rituale Romanum, Pauli V Iussu Editum, et a Benedicto XIV Auctum et Castigatum, Romae: Pustet, 1911.

Rituale Romanum, Pauli V Iussu Editum, Aliorumque Pontificum Cura Recognitum atque Auctoritate Ssmi. D.N. Pii Papae XI ad Normam Codicis Iuris Canonici Accomodatum, 4. ed. juxta typicam (1925), Ratisbonae: Pustet, 1935.

Ritual, The Priest's New, compiled by Rev. Paul Griffith, Baltimore: John Murphy, 1940.

Statuta Dioecesis Bellevillensis Lata ac Promulgata in Synodo Dioecesana Bellevillensi Quinta Die 27 Dec. 1939 Celebrata, Belleville, Illinois: Buechler Printing Co., 1940.

Synodus Diocesana Fargensis Prima, . . . A.D. 1941 Habita, Bruce: Milwauchiae, 1941.

Wilkins, D., *Concilia Magne Britanniae et Hiberniae,* 4 vols., London, 1737.

Reference Works

Aertnys J.-Damen, C. A., *Theologia Moralis,* 12. ed., 4 post codicem, 2 vols., Taurinorum Augustae: Marietti, 1932.

Alphonsus, M. de Ligouri, St., *Theologia Moralis,* cura et estudio P. Gaudé, 4 vols., Romae, 1905-1912.

Ayrinhac, H. A., *Marriage Legislation in the New Code of Canon Law,* new revised ed., New York: Benziger Bros., 1938.

(Bachofen), Charles Augustine, *A Commentary on the New Code of Canon Law,* 8 vols., Vol. V, *Marriage Law, Matrimonial Trials,* 5. ed., St. Louis, Mo.: B. Herder Book Co., 1935.

Barbosa, Augustinus, *De Officio et Potestate Episcopi,* Lugduni, 1656.

Baruffaldo, G., *Ad Rituale Romanum Commentaria,* 3 vols., Florentiae, 1817.

Bellarminus, Robertus, St., *Disputationum Roberti Bellarmini Politani, S.J. de Controversiis Christinae Fidei Tomi Quattuor,* 4 vols., Neapoli, 1856.

Benedictus XIV, *De Synodo Dioecesana,* 2 vols., Romae, 1767.

————, *Institutiones Ecclesiasticae,* 3 vols., Lovanii, 1762.

Berardi, Carolus Sebastianus, *Gratiani Canones Genuini ab Apocryphis Discreti,* 4 vols., Venetiis, 1777.

Blat, Albertus, *Commentarium Textus Codicis Iuris Canonici,* 5 vols. in 7, Vol. III, Pars I, *De Sacramentis,* 2. ed., Romae: Ex typographia Pontificia in Instituto Pii IX, 1924.

Bouscaren, T. Lincoln, *Canon Law Digest,* 2 vols. and supplement, Mil waukee: Bruce, 1934, 1937, 1941.

Brennan, *The Simple Convalidation of Marriage,* The Catholic University of America Canon Law Studies, n. 102, Washington, D. C., The Catholic University of America, 1937.

Cappello, Felix M., *Tractatus Canonico-Moralis de Sacramentis,* 3 vols. in 6, Vol. III, *De Matrimonio,* 4. ed., Romae: Apud Aedes Univ. Gregorianae, 1939.

Cerato, Prosdocimus, *Matrimonium a Codice Iuris Canonici Desumptum,* 4. ed. concordatis pro Italia legibus aucta et iuxta illas concinnata, Patavii: Libr. Gregoriana edidit typis Seminarii, 1929.

Chelodi, Joannes, *Ius Matrimoniale,* 4. ed., Tridenti: Libreria Moderna Editrice A. Ardesi, 1937.

Cicognani, Amleto, Canon Law, 2. ed., auth. English translation by J. O'Hara and F. Brennan, The Dolphin Press: Philadelphia, 1935.

Corbett, Percy A., *The Roman Law of Marriage,* Oxford: Clarendon Press, 1930.

Cronin, Charles J., *The New Matrimonial Legislation,* London, 1909.

De Becker, Iulius *De Sponsalibus et Matrimonio Praelectiones Canonicae,* Lovanii et Neo Eboraci, 2. ed., 1903.

————, *De Matrimonio Praelectiones Canonicae,* editio nova ad tramites codicis iuris canonici accomodata, Louvain: Fr. Ceuterick, 1931.

De Smet, *Tractatus, Theologico-Canonicus de Sponsalibus et Matrimonio,* 4. ed., Brugis: Car. Beyaert, 1927.

Esmein, A., *Le Mariage end Droit Canonique,* 12. ed., 2 vols. (Vol. I, rev. by R. Génestal, Vol II, rev. by R. Génestal and J. Dauvillier), Recueil Sirey: Paris, 1929-1935.

Fanfani, Ludovicus, *De Iure Parochorum,* 2. ed., Taurini-Romae: Marietti, 1936.

Feije, Henricus Joannes (also Feye), *De Impedimentis et Dispensationibus Matrimonialibus,* 3. ed., Lovanii, 1885.

————, *De Nuptiarum Benedictione,* Amstelodami, 1848.

————, *Dissertatio Canonica de Matrimoniis Mixtis,* Lovanii, 1847. Gasparri, Petrus, *Tractatus de Matrimonio,* 3. ed., 2 vols., Parisiis, 1904.

————, *Tractatus Canonicus de Matrimonio,* ed. nova ad mentem Codicis I. C., 2 vols., Romae: Typis Polyglottis Vaticanis, 1932.

Gougnard, Armand, *Tractatus de Matrimonio,* 7. ed., Mechliniae: H. Dessain., 1931.

Hinschius, Paulus, *Decretales Pseudo-Isidorianae et Capitula Angilramni,* Lipsiae, 1863.

Hostiensis (Henricus de Segusio), *Commentaria in Quinque Decretalium Libros,* 5 vols. in 3, Venetiis, 1581.

Joyce, George Hayward, *Christian Marriage,* London: Sheed & Ward, 1933.

Kenrick, Franciscus Patricius, *Theologia Moralis,* 2 vols., Mechliniae, 1861.

Martène, Edmundus, *De Antiquis Ecclesiae Ritibus,* 3 vols., Rotomagi, 1700-1702.

Migne, Jacques Paul, *Patrologiae Cursus Completus, Series Latina,* 221 vols., Parisiis, 1844-1864.

————, *Patrologiae Cursus Completus, Series Graeca,* 161 vols., Parisiis, 1856-1866.

Monacelli, F., *Formularium Fori Ecclesiastici,* 3 vols., Romae, 1844.

Nau, Louis J., *Manual on the Marriage Laws of the Code of Canon Law,* New York, Cincinnati: Pustet, 1934.

O'Kane, James, *Notes on the Rubrics of the Roman Ritual,* new ed. completely revised in accordance with the latest (1925) *editio typica* of the *Rituale Romanum,* & decrees of the Sacred Congregations, by the Rev. Michael J. Fallon, Dublin: James Duffy & Co., Ltd., 1938.

Payen, G., *De Matrimonio in Missionibus ac Potissimum in Sinis Tractatus Practicus et Casus,* 2. ed., 3 vols., Zi-ka-wei: in Typographia T'ou-se-we, 1936.

Petrovits, *The New Church Law on Matrimony,* Philadelphia, 1919.

Reiffenstuel, Anacletus, *Ius Canonicum Universum,* 5 vols. in 7, Parisiis, 1864-1870.

Rossi, Joseph, *De Matrimonii Celebratione,* Romae: Pustet, 1924.

Sanchez, Thomas, *Disputationum de Sancto Matrimonii Sacramento Tomi Tres,* Antverpiae, 1626.

Schenk, Francis J., *The Matrimonial Impediments of Mixed Religion and Disparity of Cult,* The Catholic University of America Canon Law Studies n. 51, Washington, D. C.: the Catholic University of America, 1929.

Schmalzgrueber, Franciscus, *Ius Ecclesiasticum Universum,* 5 vols. in 12, Romae, 1843-1845.

Schulte, Ioannes F., *Handbuch des katholischen Eherechts,* Giessen, 1855.

Smith, William, and Cheetham, Samuel, *Dictionary of Christian Antiquities,* 2 vols., London, 1908.

Tanquerey, Ad., *Synopsis Theologiae Moralis et Pastoralis,* 3 vols., Vol. I, *De Poenitentia, De Matrimonio et Ordine,* 12. ed., 3 post Codicem, Parisiis, Tornaci (Belg.), Romae: Desclée et Socii, 1936.

Van Hove, A., *Commentarium Lovaniense in Codicem Iuris Canonici,* Vol. I, Tom. I, *Prologomena,* Mechliniae et Romae: Dessain, 1928.

Vermeersch, Arthur, and Cruesen, J., *Epitome Iuris Canonici,* 3 vols., Mechliniae-Romae: H. Dessain, I, 6. ed., 1937; II-III, 5. ed., 1934-1936.

Villien, A., *The History and Liturgy of the Sacraments,* English translation by H. F. Edward, London: Burns, Oates & Washbourne, Ltd., 1932.

Vlaming, Th. M., *Praelectiones Iuris Matrimonii,* 3 ed., 2 vols., Bussum in Hollandia: Sumptibus Societatis Editricis Anonymae Olim Paulus Brand, 1919-1921.

Watkins, Oscar D., *Holy Matrimony,* New York, 1895.

Wernz, Franciscus X., *Ius Decretalium,* 6 vols. in 10, Vol. IV, *Ius Matrimoniale Ecclesiae Catholicae,* 2. ed., Prati, pars prima, 1911; pars secunda, 1912.

Wernz, F. X., Vidal, P., *Ius Canonicum,* 7 vols. in 8, Vol. V, *Ius Matrimoniale* Romae: Apud Aedes Universitatis Gregorianae, 1925.

Woywod, Stanislaus, *A Practical Commentary on the Code of Canon Law,* 4. ed., 2 vols., New York: Joseph F. Wagner, 1932.

Periodicals

L'Ami du Clergé, Paris-Bruxelles, 1879-1883; Bruxelles-Genève, 1883-1887; Paris, 1887-1888; Langres, 1889-

Australasian Catholic Record, The Manly N.S.W., 1924-

Archiv für katholisches Kirchenrecht, Innsbruck, 1857-1861; Main, 1862-

Irish Ecclesiastical Record, The, Dublin, 1864- ; 5th Series, 1913-

Jus Pontificium, Romae, 1921-

Neus Archiv der Gesellschaft, für ältere deutsche Geschichtskunde, 50 vols., Hanover, later Berlin, 1876-1935.

Nouvelle Revue Théologique, Paris, 1869-

Perfice Munus! Torino, 1926-

Theologisch-praktische Quartalschrift, Linz, 1832-

Articles

C. D., "De Sacramento Matrimonii,"—*Perfice Munus!,* VIII (1933), 901-905.

Hilling, "Sind Haustrauungen bei gemeischten Ehen erlaubt?"—*AKKR,* CV (1925), 111-113.

"Music at Mixed Marriages,"—*Australasian Catholic Record,* III (1926), 348.

"Notes and Queries,"—*Irish Ecclesiastical Record,* 5th series, XXXIII (1929), 61.

O'Donnell, "Sections of the New Code in Force," *Irish Ecclesiastical Record,* 5th series, X (1917, 353-366.)

Oesterle, "Circa Declarationem Authenticam Can. 1102 De Passiva Assistentia,"—*Jus Pontificium,* X (1930), 110-119, 292-314.

Planchard, "Dispense de Disparite de Culte et de Religion Mixte,"—*NRT,* XV (1883), 573-601.

"Quelle est la portée du canon 1108?"—*L'Ami du Clergé,* XLVI (1929), 10-11.

Rossi, "L'Istituto del Matrimonio in Italia dopo il Concordato Lateranense" (continuazione),—*Perfice Munus!,* VII (1932), 759-763, 836-841.

Seckel, "Studien zu Benedictus Levita,"—*Neues Archiv der Gesellschaft, für ältere deutsche Geschichtskunde,* XXXIX (1914), 393-398.

"Some Recent Decisions Concerning the Nuptial Blessing,"—*Irish Ecclesiastical Record,* 5th series, XII (1918), 419-421.

"The Meaning of Solemnities,"—*Augustralasian Catholic Record,* XV (1938), 173.

Abbreviations

AAS—*Acta Apostolicae Sedis.*
AKKR—*Archiv für katholisches Kirchenrecht.*
Decr. Auth.—*Decreta Authentica Congregationis Sacrorum Rituum,* etc.
Fontes—*Codicis Iuris Canonici Fontes cura . . . Gasparri editi.*
MGH—*Monumenta Germaniae Historica.*
MPG—Migne, *Patrologia Graeca.*
MPL—Migne, *Patrologia Latina.*
NRT—*Nouvelle Revue Théologique.*
PCI—*Pontificia Commissio Interpretationis.*
S.C.C.—Sacra Congregatio Concilii.
S.C. de Prop. Fide—Sacra Congregatio de Propaganda Fide.
S.C. de Sacr.—Sacra Congregatio de Sacramentis.
S.C.S. Off.—Sacra Congregatio Sancti Officii.
Secret. Stat.—Secretariatus Status.
S.R.C.—Sacrorum Rituum Congregatio.

BIOGRAPHICAL NOTE

Edward John Dodwell was born on July 23, 1905, in Philadelphia. After completing his high school course at West Philadelphia Catholic High School he entered Saint Charles Seminary, Overbrook. After finishing the college course, he was sent to the American College in Rome. He pursued his philosophical and theological studies at the University of the Propaganda, obtaining the degrees of Ph.D. and S.T.B. He completed his theological course at St. Mary's Seminary, Baltimore. He was ordained to the Holy Priesthood on June 3, 1939, and was sent to the Catholic University of America in September of the same year. There he entered the School of Canon Law and received the degree of the Baccalaureate in Canon Law in June, 1940, and the degree of the Licentiate in Canon Law in June, 1941.

INDEX

CANON LAW STUDIES

1. Freriks, Rev. Celestine A., C.PP.S., J.C.D., Religious Congregations in Their External Relations, 121 pp., 1916.
2. Galliher, Rev. Daniel M., O.P., J.C.D., Canonical Elections, 117 pp., 1917.
3. Borkowski, Rev. Aurelius L., O.F.M., J.C.D., De Confraternitatibus Ecclesiasticis, 136 pp., 1918.
4. Castillo, Rev. Cayo, J.C.D., Disertacion Historico-Canonica sobre la Potestad del Cabildo en Sede Vacante o Impedida del Vicario Capitular, 99 pp., 1919 (1918).
5. Kubelbeck, Rev. William J., S.T.B., J.C.D., The Sacred Pentitentiaria and Its Relations to Faculties of Ordinaries and Priests, 129 pp., 1918.
6. Petrovits, Rev. Joseph J.C., S.T.D., J.C.D., The New Church Law On Matrimony, X-461 pp., 1919.
7. Hickey, Rev. John J., S.T.B., J.C.D., Irregularities and Simple Impediments in the New Code of Canon Law, 100 pp., 1920.
8. Klekotka, Rev. Peter J., S.T.B., J.C.D., Diocesan Consultors, 179 pp., 1920.
9. Wanenmacher, Rev. Francis, J.C.D., The Evidence in Ecclesiastical Procedure Affecting the Marriage Bond, 1920 (Printed 1935).
10. Golden, Rev. Henry Francis, J.C.D., Parochial Benefices in the New Code, IV-119 pp., 1921 (Printed 1925).
11. Koudelka, Rev. Charles J., J.C.D., Pastors, Their Rights and Duties According to the New Code of Canon Law, 211 pp., 1921.
12. Melo, Rev. Antonius, O.F.M., J.C.D., De Exemptione Regularium, X-188 pp., 1921.
13. Schaaf, Rev. Valentine Theodore, O.F.M., S.T.B., J.C.D., The Cloister, X-180 pp., 1921.
14. Burke, Rev. Thomas Joseph, S.T.D., J.C.D., Competence in Ecclesiastical Tribunals, IV-117 pp., 1922.
15. Leech, Rev. George Leo, J.C.D., A Comparative Study of the Constitution, "Apostolicae Sedis" and the "Codex Juris Canonici," 179 pp., 1922.
16. Motry, Rev. Hubert Louis, S.T.D., J.C.D., Diocesan Faculties According to the Code of Canon Law, II-167 pp., 1922.
17. Murphy, Rev. George Lawrence, J.C.D., Delinquencies and Penalties in the Administration and Reception of the Sacraments, IV-121 pp., 1923.
18. O'Reilly, Rev. John Anthony, S.T.B., J.C.D., Ecclesiastical Sepulture in the New Code of Canon Law, II-129 pp., 1923.

19. Michalicka, Rev. Wenceslas Cyrill, O.S.B., J.C.D., Judicial Procedure in Dismissal of Clerical Exempt Religious, 107 pp., 1923.
20. Dargin, Rev. Edward Vincent, S.T.B., J.C.D., Reserved Cases According to the Code of Canon Law, IV-103, pp., 1924.
21. Godfrey, Rev. John A., S.T.B., J.C.D., The Right of Patronage According to the Code of Canon Law, 153 pp., 1924.
22. Hagedorn, Rev. Francis Edward, J.C.D., General Legislation on Indulgences, II-154 pp., 1924.
23. King, Rev. James Ignatius, J.C.D., The Administration of the Sacraments to Dying Non-Catholics, V-141 pp., 1924.
24. Winslow, Rev. Francis Joseph, A.F.M., J.C.D., Vicars and Prefects Apostolic, IV-149 pp., 1924.
25. Correa, Rev. Jose Servelion, S.T.L., J.C.D., La Potestad Legislativa de la Iglesia Catolica, IV-127 pp., 1925.
26. Dugan, Rev. Henry Francis, A.M., J.C.D., The Judiciary Department of the Diocesan Curia, 87 pp., 1925.
27. Keller, Rev. Charles Frederick, S.T.B., J.C.D., Mass Stipends, 167 pp., 1925.
28. Paschang, Rev. John Linus, J.C.D., The Sacramentals According to the Code of Canon Law, 129 pp., 1925.
29. Pointek, Rev. Cyrillus, O.F.M., S.T.B., J.C.D., De Indulto Exclaustrationis necnon Saecularizationis, XIII-289 pp., 1925.
30. Kearney, Rev. Richard Joseph, S.T.B., J.C.D., Sponsors at Baptism According to the Code of Canon Law, IV-127 pp., 1925.
31. Bartlett, Rev. Chester Joseph, A.M., LL.B., J.C.D., The Tenure of Parochial Property in the United States of America, V-108 pp., 1926.
32. Kilker, Rev. Adrian Jerome, J.C.D., Extreme Unction, V-425 pp., 1926.
33. McCormick, Rev. Robert Emmett, J.C.D., Confessors of Religious, VIII-266 pp., 1926.
34. Miller, Rev. Newton Thomas, J.C.D., Founded Masses According to the Code of Canon Law, VII-93 pp., 1926.
35. Roelker, Rev. Edward G., S.T.D., J.C.D., Principles of Privilege According to the Code of Canon Law, XI-166 pp., 1926.
36. Bakalarczyk, Rev. Richardus, M.I.C., J.U.D., De Novitiatu, VIII-208 pp., 1927.
37. Pizzuti, Rev. Lawrence, O.F.M., J.U.L., De Parochis Religiosis, 1927. (Not printed).
38. Bliley, Rev. Nicholas Martin, O.S.B., J.C.D., Altars According to the Code of Canon Law, XIX-132 pp., 1927.
39. Brown, Mr. Brendan Francis, A.B. LL.M., J.U.D., The Canonical Juristic Personality with Special Reference to Its Status in the United States of America, V-212 pp., 1927.

40. Cavanaugh, Rev. William Thomas, C.P., J.U.D., The Reservation of the Blessed Sacrament, VIII-101 pp., 1927.
41. Doheny, Rev. William J., C.S.C., A.B., J.U.D., Church Property: Modes of Acquisition, X-118 pp., 1927.
42. Feldhaus, Rev. Aloysius H., C.PP.S., J.C.D., Oratories, IX-141 pp., 1927.
43. Kelly, Rev. James Patrick, A.B., J.C.D., The Jurisdiction of the Simple Confessor, X-208 pp., 1927.
44. Neuberger, Rev. Nicholas J., J.C.D., Canon 6 or the Relation of the Codex Juris Canonici to the Preceding Legislation, V-95 pp., 1927.
45. O'Keefe, Rev. Gerald Michael, J.C.D., Matrimonial Dispensations, Powers of Bishops, Priests and Confessors, VIII-232 pp., 1927.
46. Quigley, Rev. Joseph A.M., A.B., J.C.B., Condemned Societies, 139 pp., 1927.
47. Zaplotnik, Rev. Johannes Leo, J.C.D., De Vicariis Foraneis, X-142 pp., 1927.
48. Duskie, Rev. John Aloysius, A.B., J.C.D., The Canonical Status of the Orientals in the United States, VIII-196 pp., 1928.
49. Hyland, Rev. Francis Edward, J.C.D., Excommunication, Its Nature, Historical Development and Effects, VIII-181 pp., 1928.
50. Reinmann, Rev. Gerald Joseph, O.M.C., J.C.D., The Third Order Secular of Saint Francis, 201 pp., 1928.
51. Schenk, Rev. Francis J., J.C.D., The Matrimonial Impediments of Mixed Religion and Disparity of Cult, XVI-318 pp., 1929.
52. Coady, Rev. John Joseph, S.T.D., J.U.D., A.M., The Appointment of Pastors, VIII-150 pp., 1929.
53. Kay, Rev. Thomas Henry, J.C.D., Competence in Matrimonial Procedure, VIII-164 pp., 1929.
54. Turner, Rev. Sidney Joseph, C.P., J.U.D., The Vow of Poverty, XLIX-217 pp., 1929.
55. Kearney, Rev. Raymond, A., A.B., S.T.D., J.C.D., The Principles, of Delegation, VII-149 pp., 1929.
56. Conran, Rev. Edward James, A.B., J.C.D., The Interdict, V-163 pp., 1930.
57. O'Neil, Rev. William H., J.C.D., Papal Rescripts of Favor, VII-218 pp., 1930.
58. Bastnagel, Rev. Clement Vincent, J.U.D., The Appointment of Parochial Adjutants and Assistants, XV-257 pp., 1930.
59. Ferry, Rev. William A., A.B., J.C.D., Stole Fees. V-135 pp., 1930.
60. Costello, Rev. John Michael, A.B., J.C.D., Domicile and Quasi-domicile, VII-201 pp., 1930.
61. Kremer, Rev. Michael Nicholas, A.B., S.T.B., J.C.D., Church Support in the United States, VI-1930.

62. Angulo, Rev. Luis, C.M., J.C.D., Legislation de la Iglesia sobre la intencion en la application de la Santa Misa, VII-104 pp., 1931.
63. Frey, Rev. Wolfgang Norbert, O.S.B., A.B., J.C.D., The Act of Religious Profession, VIII-174 pp., 1931.
64. Roberts, Rev. James Brendan, A.B., J.C.D., The Banns of Marriage, XIV-140 pp., 1931.
65. Ryder, Rev. Raymond Aloysius, A.B., J.C.D., Simony, IX-151 pp., 1931.
66. Campagna, Rev. Angelo, Ph.D., J.U.D., Il Vicario Generale del Vescovo, VII-205 pp., 1931.
67. Cox, Rev. Joseph Godfrey, A.B., J.C.D., The Administration ot Seminaries, VI-124 pp., 1931.
68. Gregory, Rev. Donald J., J.U.D., The Pauline Privilege, XV-165 pp., 1931.
69. Donohue, Rev. John F., J.C.D., The Impediment of Crime, VII-110 pp., 1931.
70. Dooley, Rev. Eugene A., O.M.I., J.C.D., Church Law On Sacred Relics, IX-143 pp., 1931.
71. Orth, Rev. Raymond Clement, O.M.C., J.C.D., The Approbation of Religious Institutes, 171 pp., 1931.
72. Pernicone, Rev. Joseph M., A.B., J.C.D., The Ecclesiastical Prohibition of Books, XII-267 pp., 1932.
73. Clinton, Rev. Connell, A.B., J.C.D., The Paschal Precept, IX-108 pp., 1932.
74. Donnelly, Rev. Francis B., A.M., S.T.L., J.C.D., The Diocesan Synod, VIII-125 pp., 1932.
75. Torrente, Rev. Camilo, C.M.F., J.C.D., Las Processiones Sagradas, V-145 pp., 1932.
76. Murphy, Rev. Edwin J., C.PP.S., J.C.D., Suspension Ex Informata Conscientia, XI-122, pp., 1932.
77. Mackenzie, Rev. Eric F., A.M., S.T.L., J.C.D., The Delict of Heresy in its Commission Penalization, Absolution, VII-124 pp., 1932.
78. Lyons Rev. Avitus E., S.T.B., J.C.D., The Collegiate Tribunal of First Instance, XI-147 pp., 1932.
79. Connolly, Rev. Thomas A., J.C.D., Appeals, XI-195 pp., 1932.
80. Sangmeister, Rev. Joseph V., A B., J.C.D., Force and Fear as Precluding Matrimonial Consent, V-211 pp., 1932.
81. Jaeger, Rev. Leo A., A.B., J.C.D., The Administration of Vacant and Quasi-vacant Episcopal Sees in the United States, IX-229 pp., 1932.
82. Rimlinger, Rev. Herbert T., J.C.D., Error Invalidating Matrimonial Consent, VII-79 pp., 1932.
83. Barrett, Rev. John D.M., S.S., J.C.D., A Comparative Study of the Third Plenary Council of Baltimore and the Code, IX-221 pp., 1932.

84. Carberry, Rev. John J., Ph.D., S.T.D., J.C.D., The Juridical Form of Marriage, X-177 pp., 1934.
85. Dolan, Rev. John L., A.B., J.C.D., The Defensor Vinculi, XII-157 pp., 1934.
86. Hannan, Rev. Jerome D., A.M., S.T.D., LL.B., J.C.D., The Canon Law of Wills, IX-517 pp., 1934.
87. Lemieux, Rev. Delisle A., A.M., J.C.D., The Sentence in Ecclesiastical Procedure, IX-131 pp., 1934.
88. O'Rourke, Rev. James J., A.B., J.C.D., Parish Registers, VII-109 pp., 1934.
89. Timlin, Rev. Bartholomew, O.F.M., A.M., J.C.D., Conditional Matrimonial Consent, X-381 pp., 1934.
90. Wahl, Rev. Francis X., A.B., J.C.D., The Matrimonial Impediments of Consanguinity and Affinity, VI-125 pp., 1934.
91. White, Rev. Robert J., A.B., LL.B., S.T.B., J.C.D., Canonical Ante-Nuptial Promises and the Civil Law, VI-152 pp., 1934.
92. Herrera, Rev. Antonio Parra, O.C.D., J.C.D., Legislation Ecclesiastica sobra el Ayuno y la Abstinencia, XI-191 pp., 1935.
93. Kennedy, Rev. Edwin J., J.C.D., The Special Matrimonial Process in Cases of Evident Nullity, X-165 pp., 1935.
94. Manning, Rev. John J., A.B., J.C.D., Presumption of Law in Matrimonial Procedure, XI-111 pp., 1935.
95. Moeder, Rev. John M., J.C.D., The Proper Bishop for Ordination and Dismissorial Letters, VII-135 pp., 1935.
96. O'Mara, Rev. William A., A.B., J.C.D., Canonical Causes For Matrimonial Dispensations, IX-155 pp., 1935.
97. Reilly, Rev. Peter, J.C.D., Residence of Pastors, IX-81 pp., 1935.
98. Smith, Rev. Mariner T., O.P., S.T.L., J.C.D., The Penal Law For Religious, VII-169 pp., 1935.
99. Whalen, Rev. Donald W., A.M., J.C.D., The Value of Testimonial Evidence in Matrimonial Procedure, XIII-297 pp., 1935.
100. Cleary, Rev. Joseph F., J.C.D., Canonical Limitations on the Alienation of Church Property, VIII-141 pp., 1936.
101. Glynn, Rev. John C., J.C.D., The Promoter of Justice, XX-337 pp., 1936.
102. Brennan, Rev. James H., S.S., A.M., S.T.B., J.C.D., The Simple Convalidation of Marriage, VI-135 pp, 1937.
103. Brunini, Rev. Joseph Bernard, J.C.D., The Clerical Obligations of Canons, 139 and 142, X-121 pp., 1937.
104. Connor, Rev. Maurice, A.B., J.C.D., The Administrative Removal of Pastors, VIII-159 pp., 1937.
105. Guilfoyle, Rev. Merlin Joseph, J.C.D., Custom, XI-144 pp., 1937.
106. Hughes, Rev. James Austin, A.B., A.M., J.C.D., Witnesses in Criminal Trials of Clerics, IX-140 pp., 1937.

107. Jansen, Rev. Raymond J., A.B., S.T.L., J.C.D., Canonical Provisions for Catechetical Instruction, VII-153 pp., 1937.
108. Kealy, Rev. John James, A.B., J.C.D,, The Introductory Libellus in Church Court Procedure, XI-121 pp., 1937.
109. McManus, Rev. James Edward, C.SS.R., J.C.D., The Administration of Temporal Goods in Religious Institutes, XVI-196 pp., 1937.
110. Moriarity, Rev. Eugene James, J.C.D., Oaths in Ecclesiastical Courts, X-115 pp., 1937.
111. Rainer, Rev. Eligius George, C.SS.R., J.C.D., Suspension of Clerics, XVII-249 pp., 1937.
112. Reilly, Rev. Thomas F., C.SS.R., J.C.D., Visitation of Religious, VI-195 pp., 1938.
113. Moriarty, Rev. Francis E., C.SS.R., J.C.D., The Extraordinary Absolution from Censures, XV-334 pp., 1938.
114. Connolly, Rev. Nicholas P., J.C.D., The Canonical Erection of Parishes, X-132 pp., 1938.
115. Donovan, Rev. James Joseph, J.C.D., The Pastor's Obligation in Prenuptial Investigation, VII-322 pp., 1938.
116. Harrigan, Rev. Robert J., M.A., S.T.B., J.C.D., The Radical Sanation of Invalid Marriages, VIII-208 pp., 1938.
117. Boffa, Rev. Conrad Humbert, J.C.D., Canonical Provisions for Catholic Schools, VII-211 pp., 1939.
118. Parsons, Rev. Anscar John, O.M. Cap., J.C.D., Canonical Elections, XII-236 pp., 1939.
119. Reilly, Rev. Edward Michael, A.B., J.C.D., The General Norms of Dispensation, X-156 pp., 1939.
120. Ryan, Rev. Gerald Aloysius, A.B., J.C.D., Principles of Episcopal Jurisdiction, XII-172 pp., 1939.
121. Burton, Rev. Francis James, C.S.C., A.B., J.C.D., A Commentary on Canon 1125, X-222 pp., 1940.
122. Miaskiewicz, Rev. Francis Sigismund, J.C.D., Supplied Jurisdiction according to Canon 209, XII-340 pp., 1940.
123. Rice, Rev. Patrick William, A.B., J.C.D., Proof of Death in Prenuptial Investigation, VIII-156 pp., 1940.
124. Anglin, Rev. Thomas Francis, M.S., J.C.D., The Eucharistic Fast, VIII-183 pp., 1941.
125. Coleman, Rev. John Jerome, J.C.D., The Minister of Confirmation, VI-153 pp., 1941.
126. Downs, Rev. John Emmanuel, A.B., J.C.D., The Concept of Clerical Immunity.
127. Esswein, Rev. Anthony Albert, J.C.D., Extrajudicial Penal Powers of Ecclesiastical Superiors, X-144 pp., 1941.

128. Farrell, Rev. Benjamin Francis, M.A., S.T.L., J.C.D., The Rights and Duties of the Local Ordinary Regarding Congregations of Women Religious of Pontifical Approval, V-195 pp., 1941.
129. Feeney, Rev. Thomas John, A.B., S.T.L., J.C.D., Restitution in Integrum, VI-169 pp., 1941.
130. Findlay, Rev. Stephen William, O.S.B., A.B., J.C.D., Canonical Norms Governing the Deposition and Degradation of Clerics.
131. Goodwine, Rev. John, A.B., S.T.L., J.C.D., The Right of the Church to Acquire Property, VIII-119 pp., 1941.
132. Heston, Rev. Edward Louis, C.S.C., PhD., S.T.D., J.C.D., The Alienation of Church Property in the United States, XII-222 pp., 1941.
133. Hogan, Rev. James John, S.T.L., J.C.D., Judicial Advocates and Procurators, VIII-200 pp., 1941.
134. Kealy, Rev. Thomas M. A.B., Litt.B., J.C.D., Dowry of Women Religious, IX-152 pp., 1941.
135. Keene, Rev. Michael James, O.S.B., J.C.D., Religious Ordinaries and Canon 198.
136. Kerin, Rev. Charles A., S.S., M.A., S.T.B., J.C.D., The Privation of Christian Burial, XVI-279 pp., 1941.
137. Louis, Rev. William Francis, M.A., J.C.D., Diocesan Archives, X-101 pp., 1941.
138. McDevitt, Rev. Gilbert Joseph, A.B., J.C.D., Legitimacy and Legitimation.
139. McDonough, Rev. Thomas Joseph, A.B., J.C.D., Apostolic Administrators.
140. Meier, Rev. Carl Anthony, A.B., J.C.D., Penal Administrative Procedure Against Negligent Pastors, XI-240 pp., 1941.
141. Schmidt, Rev. John Rogg, A.B., J.C.D., The Principles of Authentic Interpretation in Canon 17 of the Code of Canon Law, XII-331 pp., 1941.
142. Slafkosky, Rev. Andrew eLonard, A.B., J.C.D., The Canonical Episcopal Visitation of the Diocese, X-197 pp., 1941.
143. Swoboda, Rev. Innocent Robert, O.F.M., J.C.D., Ignorance in Relation to the Imputability of Delicts, IX-271 pp., 1941.
144. Dubé, Rev. Arthur Joseph, A.B., J.C.D., The General Principles for the Reckoning of Time in Canon Law. VIII-299 pp., 1941.
145. McBride, Rev. James T., A.B., J.C.D., Incardination and Excardination of Seculars., XX-585 pp., 1941.
146. Król, Rev. John J., J.C.L., The Defendant in Contentious Trials, IX-207 pp., 1942.
147. Comyns, Rev. Joseph J., C.SS.R., J.C.L., The Papal and Episcopal Administration of Church Property.
148. Barry, Rev. Garrett Francis, O.M.I., J.C.L., Violation of the Cloister.

149. Bolduc, Rev. Gatien, C.S.V., A.B., S.T.L., J.C.L., Les études dans les religions cléricales.
150. Boyle, Rev. David John, M.A., J.C.L., The Juridic Effects of Moral Certitude on Pre-Nuptial Guarantees.
151. Canavan, Rev. Walter Joseph, M.A., Litt.D., J.C.L., Profession of Faith.
152. Desrochers, Rev. Bruno, A.B., Ph.L., S.T.B., J.C.L., Le Premier Concile Plénier de Québec et le Code de Droit Canonique.
153. Dillon, Rev. Robert Edward, A.B., J.C.L., Common Law Marriage.
154. Dodwell, Rev. Edward John, Ph.D., S.T.B., J.C.L., The Time and Place for the Celebration of Marriage.
155. Donnellan, Rev. Thomas Andrew, A.B., J.C.L., The Obligation of the Missa pro Populo.
156. Eltz, Rev. Louis Anthony, A.B., JC.L., Cooperation in Crime.
157. Gass, Rev. Sylvester Francis, M.A., J.C.L., Ecclestiastical Pensions.
158. Guiniven, Rev. John Joseph, C.SS.R., J.C.L., The Precept of Hearing Mass on Sundays and Holy Days of Obligation.
159. Gulczynski, Rev. John Theophilus, J.C.L., The Desecration and Violation of Churches.
160. Hammill, Rev. John Leo, M.A., J.C.L., The Obligations of the Traveler according to Canon 14.
161. Haydt, Rev. John Joseph, A.B., J.C.L., Reserved Benefices.
162. Huser, Rev. Roger John, O.F.M., A.B., J.C.L., The Crime of Abortion in Canon Law.
163. Kearney, Rev. Francis Patrick, A.B., S.T.L., J.C.L., The Principles of Canon 1127.
164. Linahen, Rev. Leo James, S.T.L., J.C.L., De Absolutione Complicis in Peccato Turpi.
165. McCloskey, Rev. Joseph Aloysius, A.B., J.C.L., The Subject of Ecclesiastical Law according to Canon 12.
166. O'Neill, Rev. Francis Joseph, C.SS.R., J.C.L., The Dismissal of Religious in Temporary Vows.
167. Prince, Rev. John Edward, A.B., S.T.B., J.C.L., The Diocesan Chancellor.
168. Riesner, Rev. Albert Joseph, C.SS.R., J.C.L., Apostates and Fugitives from Religious Institutes.
169. Stenger, Rev. Joseph Bernard, J.C.L., The Mortgaging of Church Property.
170. Waldron, Rev. Joseph Francis, A.B., J.C.L., The Minister of Baptism.
171. Willett, Rev. Robert Albert, J.C.L., The Probative Value of Documents in Ecclesiastical Trials.
172. Woeber, Rev. Edward Martin, M.A., J.C.L., The Interpellations.

www.ingramcontent.com/pod-product-compliance
Lightning Source LLC
LaVergne TN
LVHW050226080826
844660LV00012B/477

* 9 7 8 0 8 1 3 2 2 3 4 3 8 *